Strengths-Based Care Management for Older Adults

Strengths-Based Care Management for Older Adults

By
Becky Fast, M.S.W., M.P.A.
&
Rosemary Chapin, Ph.D.

HEALTH
PROFESSIONS
PRESS

Baltimore • London • Winnipeg • Sydney

Health Professions Press, Inc.
Post Office Box 10624
Baltimore, Maryland 21285-0624

www.healthpropress.com

Typesetting by A.W. Bennett, Inc., Hartland, Vermont.
Printed in the United States of America by Versa Press, Inc., East Peoria, Illinois.

Library of Congress Cataloging-in-Publication Data
Fast, Becky.
    Strengths-based care management for older adults / Becky Fast and Rosemary Chapin.
      p. cm.
    Includes bibliographical references and index.
    ISBN 1-878812-60-2
    1. Aged—Home care. 2. Aged—Long-term care. 3. Caregivers. I. Chapin, Rosemary
    Kennedy. II. Title.

HV1451.F39 2000
362.6—dc21
                                               00-021494

British Cataloguing in Publication Data are available from the British Library.

Contents

Preface

Case/care management has gained recognition for its effectiveness in delaying, and sometimes preventing, the placement of older adults and adults with disabilities in nursing facilities. With this recognition, many states have instituted home- and community-based service programs as an option for people with ongoing illnesses or disabilities who otherwise would be forced into institutional settings. As the long-term care system moves toward home care, older adults with ongoing health problems are increasingly asking for a larger array of medically oriented services.

Reflecting these needs, the national trend within the field of aging and long-term care services has been to expand client direction of services. Strengths-based care management meshes with this trend in a number of ways: 1) it places more control and direction into the hands of clients, 2) it discovers and mobilizes client strengths to enhance self-reliance, and 3) it addresses the importance of medical, mental health, and social support services.

Dr. Charles Rapp and Dr. Ronna Chamberlain at the University of Kansas School of Social Welfare developed the strengths model of care management in the early 1980s for people with severe and persistent mental illness (Rapp & Chamberlain, 1985). The National Institute of Mental Health soon recognized the model as one of the leading care management models for people with mental illness.

Care management is an evolving discipline. The literature continues to examine the effectiveness of using a strengths-based approach with vulnerable populations, including older adults receiving long-term care and home health care, children with severe emotional disturbance, adults with mental illness, and people with substance abuse problems (Cowger, 1994; DeJong & Miller, 1995; Fast & Chapin, 1996; Perkins & Tice, 1995; Poertner & Ronnau, 1990; Pray, 1992; Rapp, Siegal, Fisher, & Wagner, 1992; Rapp & Wintersteen, 1989; Saleebey, 1992; Sullivan, 1989; Sullivan & Fisher, 1994). The first practice text, *The Strengths Model: Case Management with People Suffering from Severe and Persistent Mental Illness*, by Dr. Charles Rapp, was published in 1998.

Through our teaching and training experiences, it became apparent that a trainer's manual was needed to accompany our learning activities and participant handouts. This manual was developed specifically to assist administrators who need help training their staff in a strengths-based approach to care management with older adults. This training manual is designed specifically for professionals working with home- and community-based older adults to increase their understanding of care management from a strengths approach. This book is primarily a trainer's guide and applies the strengths model of care management to people who often are viewed as very frail and vulnerable.

About the Authors

Becky Fast, M.S.W., M.P.A., is Coordinator of Constituent Casework Services for U.S. Representative Dennis Moore of Kansas's Third Congressional District. She joined Congressman Moore's staff in 1999 after serving as an adjunct professor and Manager of Long-Term Care Research and Training in the School of Social Welfare at the University of Kansas. She holds master's degrees in social work and public administration from the University of Kansas.

Fast has developed numerous training programs specifically on the strengths perspective for social work students and care managers working with older adults. In addition, she has designed and delivered specialized training workshops on elder abuse, dementia, and mental illness for field staff with the Kansas Department on Aging and the Kansas Department of Social and Rehabilitation Services.

During her tenure at the University of Kansas, Fast conducted, in collaboration with the state Medicaid agency, several program evaluations of state-funded nursing facility and home- and community-based services. She also has taught gerontology and care management courses at both the undergraduate and graduate levels and has presented at national and international in-service seminars and conferences. Ms. Fast has direct client experience in a nursing facility and a home health care agency and in hospital care.

Rosemary Chapin, Ph.D., is Associate Professor in the University of Kansas School of Social Welfare. She received a Ph.D. in Social Work from the University of Minnesota. Dr. Chapin has extensive teaching, research, policy, and program development experience in the long-term care arena. She worked for 5 years for the Minnesota Department of Human Services in their long-term care unit, where her responsibilities included research and development of innovative long-term initiatives.

Use of the strengths perspective in policy development and long-term care management is an important component of Dr. Chapin's teaching and research. She has been involved in researching and providing training and technical assistance to help craft more effective state long-term care practices. Projects have included piloting a system for expediting home- and community-based service delivery to frail older adults at risk for nursing facility placement, evaluating the nursing facility preadmission screening program, collaborating with state staff to develop a community reentry program for high-functioning nursing facility residents, and developing and delivering training for long-term care case managers.

Acknowledgments

This manual would never have been developed if Dr. Charles Rapp, Associate Dean and Professor of the School of Social Welfare at the University of Kansas, and one of the developers of the strengths model of care management, had not asked us to apply his work to older adults. His belief in our ability to do this work was a gift that we will never forget. His ability to tap into our hidden strengths has forever sold us on the restorative power of helping people by using a strengths-based approach.

We are particularly grateful to the social work students at the University of Kansas School of Social Welfare in Lawrence and the human services majors at Washburn University in Topeka, who applied the strengths model and responded with meaningful suggestions. We also thank the Medicaid waiver care managers and Area Agency on Aging care managers who supported the development of this training program by applying the strengths perspective in their daily practice with older adults.

Finally, we would like to thank our colleagues at the University of Kansas School of Social Welfare: co-trainer Diane McDiarmid for providing us with training information from her experience using the strengths model with people with severe and persistent mental illness; Wally Kisthardt for his contribution to the development of the strengths model and subsequent training activities, and Jan Moore for her willingness to edit our many drafts.

It is our hope that this training program contributes to a richer understanding of how older adults can demonstrate remarkable resiliency, even within the context of disabling health problems.

For the Trainer

The strengths approach provides techniques and tools to help care managers focus on clients' strengths and abilities instead of their pathology, illnesses, or problems. Care managers identify clients' strengths and create situations in which clients can use their abilities to achieve personal goals. The strengths model is grounded in the belief that change can happen only when one collaborates with an individual's aspirations, perceptions, and strengths.

Care managers' focusing on older adults' strengths and capabilities helps clients gain a sense of control over their lives and motivation. Clients are viewed as competent and able to participate in the planning and delivery processes of the care plan. They experience renewed self-confidence and independence as care managers move with them in directions that the clients themselves choose and in areas in which they feel capable and willing. Clients are viewed as experts in defining their own needs, and the role of the care manager changes to reflect a greater appreciation of clients' expertise.

The strengths perspective "requires us to identify (for ourselves, for others, and for the people with whom we work) the abilities they possess which may not be obvious, even to themselves . . . It is always easier to see what is wrong, and what people lack. Empowering research (and practice) attempts to identify what is right with people, and what resources are already available, so as to encourage their use and expansion." (Rappaport, 1990, p. 12)

Training Goals and Expectations

Strengths-Based Care Management for Older Adults is designed to increase group participants' understanding of care management practice, including roles and responsibilities; value components; and specific skill development such as interviewing, assessment, care planning, and client advocacy. As a trainer, it is as important for you to ask the participants what they expect to gain from the training as it is to specify what you hope they will gain. Unless you begin the modules by clarifying the purpose and goals of the training, participants with unmet expectations will become dissatisfied as the training unfolds. Usually, adult learners are more ready to learn when mutual expectations and goals are communicated from the start.

The overall purpose of the training program is to provide direct service providers with information, ideas, affirmation, and opportunities to have fun during the learning process. What do information, ideas, and affirmation mean to trainers in terms of the strengths approach?

- Information—To increase practice knowledge and skills for working with older people from a strengths perspective
- Ideas—To provide tangible ideas, techniques, and specific tools for meeting the diverse helping needs that confront care managers daily
- Affirmation—To give care managers a sense of excitement about their work, which re-affirms their purpose, and to help care managers and supervisors reflect on how to enhance their own practice skills and methods

On completion of the training modules, participants are expected to achieve five primary objectives:

1. Articulate a conceptual understanding of strengths-based care management practice
2. Define the core values underlying the strengths model of practice
3. Identify strategies for establishing a successful client–care manager relationship
4. Demonstrate the application of selected strengths-based care management skills (e.g., engagement, strengths assessment, goal planning) to an older adult client seeking social services
5. Describe effective advocacy and resource acquisition strategies for working collaboratively with community agencies and informal supports

Your self-awareness is necessary to ensure that participants receive the training they want. As a trainer, think through your expectations for your training participants with the following commonly held beliefs in mind:

- Real learning occurs when trainees ask questions, challenge one another, and raise problems and issues that emerge during training.
- Successful training depends on group participation during discussions and learning activities.
- Real learning occurs when participants are willing to suspend their disbelief or cynicism and become engaged in trying new ideas and practice methods.

Using This Training Manual

This book provides an overview of the strengths approach to care management with older adults through a collection of exercises. To use the instructional methods included in this manual effectively, it is imperative that you have sufficient knowledge of the strengths model of care management. The authors strongly recommend supplementing the 20 learning units with information and/or practice techniques from our chapter in Dr. Dennis Saleebey's *The Strengths Perspective in Social Work Practice* (1997) and our 1996 article in the *Journal of Case Management,* "The Strengths Model in Long-Term Care: Linking Cost Containment and Consumer Empowerment." Dr. Charles Rapp's book *The Strengths Model: Case Management with Severe and Persistent Mental Illness* (1998) contains useful background information on the concepts that are illustrated in the learning activities. Additional reference materials that you can draw on are listed in the reference section at the back of the book.

Although primarily designed for newly employed care managers or individuals who are interested in pursuing employment in care management, each unit can be enhanced for advanced practitioners by applying the core concepts to more challenging care situations during the group discussions and learning activities. This book is appropriate for training a variety of long-term care professionals, including nurses, social workers, family caregivers, and students preparing for a career in aging issues.

When using this manual as a formal training tool with a large group of participants, the authors suggest the following:

- The activities work best with a group that is no larger than 25–30 people and in settings that allow for a U-shaped seating arrangement.
- Three 8-hour days (including 90 minutes for breaks and lunch) are needed to adequately cover all of the material in the book.
- Adult learning is best accomplished when didactic presentations are limited to 30 minutes and followed by interactive activities or discussions.
- Discussion and feedback should always be encouraged. It is important to engage trainees by asking for their opinions and experiences.
- Adult learners tend to want to learn only what they need to know to cope effectively with their day-to-day responsibilities. Case examples—real life or simulated—should be incorporated into each and every learning session.
- A variety of audiovisual media such as overhead transparencies and flipcharts should be used throughout the training sessions to highlight important points generated by the group. By using a variety of audiovisual techniques, the trainees' diverse learning styles can be addressed.

This extremely flexible manual can be used in a variety of courses and with different training formats and styles. The learning units can be used as a complete training program or each unit can be used individually to enliven classroom discussions, in-services, and continuing education workshops.

The manual is divided into five modules, and each module is divided into several "learning units." Each module contains an introduction that provides background information for the subsequent learning activities. Each learning unit includes: 1) a statement of purpose that delineates what you should teach and what should be mastered by the participants, 2) the approximate amount of time that is required to complete the exercise, 3) instructions to guide you in developing and presenting the unit, and 4) learning activities. The learning activities include presenter's points, discussion guides, and exercises that apply the concepts that are presented.

Module 1 explores the values and beliefs that guide and direct the delivery of strengths-based care management practice. Group exercises facilitate the application of strengths principles to actual practice.

Module 2 paints a picture of effective helping partnerships and the engagement process. Strategies for developing trust and rapport to ensure a successful client–care manager relationship are outlined.

Module 3 presents an alternative to the traditional long-term care functional assessment process. The essential components of a strengths assessment process are introduced and demonstrated by using the strengths inventory tool. Small-group activities help participants to use strengths-based assessment techniques.

Module 4 segues from identifying hidden strengths and resources to helping clients use their strengths in creating goal plans. Training focuses on the importance of setting goals, creating standards for effective goal planning, and establishing methods to ensure successful goal completion. The personal goal planning tool is presented, and participants practice using the tool in pairs (dyads). Participants are asked to develop a personal goal plan with a partner based on the information that is given to them.

Module 5 concludes the training program with activities and information on advocacy methods and strategies for influencing informal and formal providers to be more responsive to the needs of older adults. Ideas for effectively identifying and recruiting informal helpers are provided. Approaches for developing and building naturally occurring helping networks and creating new community resources are explored through case examples.

Strengths Principles and Functions

The strengths model operates on the premise that older people have a tremendous capacity for continued growth and autonomy. This belief requires continual attention to individual experiences, talents, and aspirations. Because each person is unique, the strengths perspective assumes that each person is the expert in defining his or her own needs or will, with the help of a care manager, get to know what he or she needs most to achieve well-being (Weick, 1984).

The helping behaviors of the strengths model differ in a number of ways from those of traditional practice. For example, traditional models have placed emphasis on identifying and solving problems. The resulting treatment strategies emerge from categories of illness, pathology, and problems rather than a pursuit of knowledge of the ways in which the person is experiencing a particular situation.

In medical and rehabilitative models old age is a disease, and aging is a medical problem that can be alleviated, if not eliminated. Services are prescribed on the basis of a medical condition rather than on the individual's unique psychological, social, spiritual, and physical needs (Pray, 1992). The diagnostic endeavor fails "to reveal the meaning of that person's struggle [and] the strengths that lie hidden in that person's story" (Weick, Rapp, Sullivan, & Kisthardt, 1989, p. 350). As a result, medical models tend to neglect broader social and psychological needs, such as housing, socialization, and transportation, which may enable people to preserve independence and dignity.

Older people traditionally are thought to be unable to take care of themselves because of pathology, illness, and deficits. Traditional treatment plans focus attention on what must be done or can be done instead of reinforcing what people can and are already doing (Rathbone-McCuan, 1992). The strengths approach stresses awareness of strengths amidst advancing cognitive and physical changes. It views disease, illness, and activity deficits as only one part of the picture and not the most important part. Problems become a backdrop rather than the foreground of the client–care manager relationship. The client is perceived as having a range of experiences, characteristics, and roles that determine who he or she is, rather than as someone who is old, disabled, or chronically ill.

Most older people have managed to survive, sometimes against great challenges and odds, before entering the care management relationship. The care manager can explore and build on that knowledge. Older people have "vast, often untapped and frequently unappreciated reservoirs of physical, emotional, cognitive, interpersonal, social, and spiritual energies which are invaluable to constructing the possibility of change, transformation, and hope" (Saleebey, 1992, p. 2).

Dependence can foster low self-esteem, depression, hopelessness, and feelings of incompetence, which can accelerate the onset of illness (Rodin & Langer, 1980). Strengths-based processes help to counter such effects by stressing the capacities that a person retains (e.g., the abilities to maintain oneself or one's home). The client–care manager relationship is one of the most important tools of the strengths model. Through it, the care manager is able to help the client bring about the changes that are needed for him or her to continue living at home or in the community. This relationship is fundamental to nurturing the client's potential for learning and change and to identifying personal and environmental resources.

The strengths approach is implemented through mutual participation and decision making among clients, caregivers, and the care manager. The traditional expert–nonexpert relationship is replaced by one of collaboration and mutual responsibility. No matter how physically or mentally impaired the older person is, he or she is capable of some degree of involvement. In most cases the person can participate far more than expected if given time and patience on the part of the caregiver. Ultimately, it is the older adult who must live out the consequences of any actions taken (Lowry, 1991).

The strengths perspective enables older people to feel in control of their lives, to solve their own problems, and to make choices for themselves, thus decreasing the likelihood of unnecessary dependence and learned helplessness. Theoretical and empirical literature support the premise that older people will experience a higher quality of life if they perceive that they have choices and control over their lives. Increased choice and control have been associated with increased feelings of independence and self-sufficiency (Ory, Abeles, & Lipman, 1991).

The strengths model assumes that people can influence their lives and their choices. Strengths model care management enhances older people's sense of control by compensating for what they cannot do. The process begins at initial contact by engaging older adults in identifying their strengths and encouraging them to develop and direct their care plan.

A strengths perspective enables practitioners to redefine and reframe their language and attitudes: from pathology to strengths, from problems to challenges and opportunities, from a preoccupation with the past to a vision of the future, and from a role as expert to a role as a collaborator. Transformation begins when the fullness of human capacity is realized in attitudes, language, and actions. The strengths model of care management is an important vehicle for this journey.

Get-Acquainted Exercise: *When I Am 80*

Purpose:
To enable participants and trainers to get to know one another and to build trust within the group

Approximate Time Required:
45 minutes (depends on the size of your group)

Supplies:
5 × 8 inch blank index cards, pens or pencils, flipchart or chalkboard, and marker or chalk

Instructions:
1. Distribute 5 × 8 index cards and pens or pencils. Ask trainees to write the following information on their card:
   • Their name, their job title, and where they are from
   • A strength they bring to the training
2. Ask trainees to close their eyes and visualize themselves at age 80. Ask the following questions:
   • Where will you be living?
   • What will you be doing?
   • What will you look like?
3. Give the trainees about 5 minutes to jot down their answers to the questions. Then go around the group and ask each participant to share his or her biographical information and how each visualizes him- or herself as an 80-year-old person. Record participant strengths on a flipchart or chalkboard.
4. Summarize all of the factors that the group members associated with <u>successful</u> aging. Specifically mention social supports, participation in activities, and personal and external strengths that group members shared. The group members' understanding of characteristics that will contribute to their own successful aging should be identified as the same factors that support healthy aging in their clients.
5. Conclude the activity by discussing why effective practice depends on care managers' coming to terms with their future selves, and how care managers must be able to confront their own feelings about growing old. Group members should understand how coming to terms with their own aging process is a critical precept to help older adults confront age-related physical and mental health changes.

Identifying Strengths

**Learning
Unit 2**

Purpose:
To identify and define our strengths and our clients' strengths

Approximate Time Required:
30 minutes

Supplies:
Flipchart, chalkboard, or overhead projector; markers or chalk; make photocopies of the handout "Defining Strengths" (see p. 15)

Instructions:
1. Distribute copies of the handout "Defining Strengths." Using the responses from Learning Unit 1, discuss the number of participant responses that fall under the listed categories.
2. Discuss the handout "Defining Strengths." Explore with participants any additional strengths categories that they have observed from their personal or professional life.
3. Conclude Learning Unit 2 by stressing that care managers who operate from a strengths approach would assess the presence of social activities, relationships, basic life necessities, and components of emotional/physical well-being as positive examples of successful aging. These strengths would be understood as opportunities on which to capitalize in the care-planning process to improve clients' quality of life.

Self-Assessment

**Learning
Unit 3**

Purpose:
To help participants assess and reflect on the primary values and beliefs embodied in strengths-based care management with older adults

Approximate Time Required:
45 minutes

Supplies:
Sticky notepads (e.g., Post-it™ Notes) or adhesive colored dots, and flipchart; make photocopies of the handout "Self-Assessment Guide" (see p. 16)

Instructions:

1. Ask participants to take one sticky notepaper or dot for every value statement that is displayed on the flipchart. On the flipchart, write all or only a few of the value statements from the handout, leaving room for participants to voice their opinions by attaching the sticky notes or dots to the newsprint pad on the flipchart.

2. Introduce the activity by telling participants that they are going to evaluate where each of them stands in relationship to the statements that are listed on the board and what the basis is for each person's position.

3. Distribute the handout. For each of the statements, ask participants to assess their position, and then place a sticky notepaper or dot at whichever end of the continuum coincides with their position—agree or disagree. Remind participants that they should not attempt to figure out the "correct" answer (there is no *correct* answer), but instead focus on determining their level of agreement or disagreement with each statement.

4. Some participants may be resistant to taking a position on a statement and may want to place their notepaper or dot in the middle of the continuum. This exercise works best when participants take a definite agree or disagree stance on the value statements. Encourage them to go with their gut reaction and not overanalyze the terminology that is used in the statements.

5. Ask for volunteers to share their responses to the items with which they disagreed and to explain the basis for their opinion. Encourage participants who agreed with the particular statement to share their opinions with the group as well.

6. Following the discussion, explain to the group that the values reflected in the statements form the foundation and basis for work using a strengths-based approach. Let the participants know that the principles will be discussed in more detail and specificity during the next training session.

Note to the Trainer

The statements were written so as to facilitate a lively and interesting discussion and to encourage participant self-reflection. The statements do not have an absolute answer. For example, a care manager may have to override a client's wishes if the person is harming him- or herself or others. Once again, no right answer exists for the first value statement. The care manager may have to start with the caregiver's view of the situation if the client is absorbed by a crisis. It is important that the trainer be mindful of situations or exceptions that elicit disagreement from participants.

7. Conclude the activity by reassuring participants that full agreement with the value statements is not expected at this time. As the training progresses, the participants should understand the rationale behind the principles and find more common ground with the principles.

Applying the Strengths Principles

Learning Unit 4

Purpose:
To assist participants in applying the strengths principles to their care management practice

Approximate Time Required:
60 minutes

Supplies:
Several notepads and pencils or pens; make photocopies of the handout "Strengths Model Principles" (see p. 17)

Instructions:
1. Use the discussion points that follow to present the basis for each principle, and illustrate each principle with concrete case examples.
2. During the presentation, highlight participants' comments from the self-assessment exercise in Learning Unit 3. Incorporate the strengths and resources that were identified by participants in Learning Units 1 and 2.
3. Ask the participants to describe in what ways they have observed the principles being applied within their individual agencies. Encourage participants to start thinking about how their agency could do business differently if these principles were applied more universally within their organizational structures.
4. Participants should form small groups of 3–4 people and select someone to record the responses. Each group should 1) list specific practices that reflect strengths-based practice in their agencies, and 2) list possible behaviors and actions in the agency's practice that could be changed to better demonstrate a strengths-based orientation.
5. After 15–20 minutes, bring the groups back together and ask each recorder to share his or her group's responses.

Discussion Points:

The strengths approach is based on five principles that guide the way in which care managers work with older people and view their participation in the helping process. The strengths principles give purpose, meaning, and direction to the helping process. The five principles are as follows:

Principle 1: Discovering and building on strengths rather than problems facilitates hope and self-reliance.

Focusing on older people's strengths, interests, and abilities rather than their disabilities, illnesses, and problems enhances their ability to move from dependence to healthy interdependence. In the strengths model problems and needs are not ignored; they are perceived as barriers to what people want. Working from a strengths perspective is much more than reframing the problem. The care manager focuses on what clients want and need by using their personal and environmental strengths.

A person's needs may not be the same as his or her wants. An elderly man may want to continue living in his home but refuses public-funded services to fix the leak in his roof. A skilled care manager would draw on his family resources and his background as a building contractor to identify free community helpers to meet his needs while capitalizing on what he wants for his life. As loss of health and functional disabilities become pronounced with age, many older adults accept the stigmatizing and confines of what they should and should not do as an older person. Subsequently, strengths are easily overlooked in the process of defining the presenting issues (Motenko & Greenberg 1995). Instead of asking, "What is wrong with this individual?" a more empowering question is, "What are the strengths that have helped this person to survive?" This question will elicit what the older person has done, can do, and already is doing to live independently.

Principle 2: Older people have the power to learn, grow, and change.

Central to this principle is the belief in older people's inherent capacity, amidst advancing age, recurring illnesses, and disability, to fulfill their dreams, aspirations, and goals in all areas of life. A care practice that focuses on this principle recognizes older adults' untapped possibilities and their capability to learn, to heal, and to better their lives. Like all human beings, sometimes clients have a hard time knowing what they want and what direction they want to go in. Helping clients learn to dream is critical to the change process. Placing artificial ceilings on clients' dreams because they are 80, 85, or 90 stifles their ability to want to learn, grow, and change.

An older woman may choose to remain living in her own home instead of moving to an apartment near the central business district. In making this choice, she must learn to use public transportation with a walker because her driver's license was revoked. She deserves the chance to make it work for her and the right to possibly fail at getting to medical appointments and the grocery store and satisfying other basic needs. Negative expectations from the care manager and caregivers can have a profound influence on her capacity to learn, grow, and change. Your belief that clients want to change rather than resist it helps to prevent them from becoming preoccupied with past deficits and directs efforts to help toward the future.

Principle 3: Relationship building is essential and primary to effectively help clients.

This principle emphasizes the importance of developing and nurturing the client–care manager relationship as a prerequisite to success. Traditional brokerage models in long-term care assume that care management can be effective without developing a trusting relationship. The broker model includes minimal client contact, with emphasis on service arrangement. A close collaborative relationship that is built on mutual trust, honesty, and openness requires smaller caseloads.

Service linkages are difficult to maintain unless the care manager has taken the time to build the relationship, explore relevant issues, provide supportive counseling, and involve the client in all care decisions. Furthermore, the relationship between the care manager and the client enhances the transfer of knowledge and skills to further develop the client's self-care capacity.

Clients often refer to their care manager as their "friend." The care manager is paid to be friendly and to help them reach their goals, but not to be their friend. Care managers should routinely ask themselves, "What is the purpose of this relationship?" and "Why am I involved in this person's life?" Survey after survey has noted that older people expect and want a relationship with their care managers.

Principle 4: Older people can participate in decisions, make choices, and determine the direction of the helping process.

Client choice and self-determination are central to this principle. The assumption is that no matter how impaired an older person, he or she is capable of some level of involvement and participation in the helping relationship. This principle addresses how needs and goals are defined in a client–care management relationship and by whom. Older adults have the right to determine the form, direction, and substance of the care management help they receive.

Strengths-based care managers focus on developing a partnership with clients and encourage shared decision making. As a result, clients know they are "in this together" with their care manager, and they assume more ownership of the process. The goal of this principle is to begin where the client is and move with him or her to his or her highest possible level of participation. The care manager's aim is to expand client confidence in making crucial decisions, such as when to seek care, what options to select, and when to move to higher levels of self-directed decision making.

In traditional service models the care management professional usually conducts an assessment and recommends strategies, and the client must either accept the recommended services or seek help elsewhere. In the strengths model, through collaborative assessment and planning, the care management professional is viewed as the agent, the adviser, or a consultant.

Older adults facing disabling health conditions often choose not to be the director of the helping process; however, opportunities still should be sought to actively give them the choice to be involved in this process. Even clients with dementia and mental health–related disabilities should be afforded as many choices as possible. The care manager's challenge is to be aware of clients' rights and the real limitations of their physical and mental conditions.

Principle 5:   Resource acquisition includes assertive outreach to all community resources.

According to this principle, the entire community is viewed as full of resources. Aggressive outreach is the preferred mode of intervention for care management services. The strengths perspective challenges the notion that only formal, paid services exist for those who can afford them, and the community is perceived as a reservoir of untapped potential possibilities. Resource acquisition taps into the naturally occurring helpers that exist in every older person's environment, such as neighbors, apartment managers, youth groups, and civic organizations.

The community is seen not as an obstacle but as an oasis of potential collaborators and a reservoir of possibilities. The primary task of the care manager is to find or rejuvenate existing resources. Care managers tend to limit their clients to accessing only formal resources. Using only formal providers cannot fully satisfy older people's emotional and social needs or deliver the individualized care that reflects a lifetime of shared values and experiences. Specialized services have been and always will be limited.

Conceptual Differences

Purpose:

To help participants understand the difference between traditional long-term care practice models and the strengths approach to care management practice

Approximate Time Required:

30 minutes

Supplies:

Make overhead transparencies and photocopies of the handouts "Models of Helping" and "Strengths Model versus Medical Models of Practice" (see pp. 18 and 19)

Instructions:

1. Briefly review the core components of the traditional medical-rehabilitative model of practice, and discuss why it is the predominant model of care management practice by using the discussion points listed below.
2. Describe how the strengths model of practice contrasts with traditional medical models of practice. Ask the following questions of participants:
    •"As you look over the two models of helping, in what ways do the models conceptualize helping differently? Does one of the models seem to be more in line with your practice notions? If so, how?"
    • "From your experience, which model or philosophy do you see used more often?"

Discussion Points:

1. Care management, like social work and other helping professions, has constructed much of its theory and practice around the assumption that people become clients because they have deficits and problems. Linear thinking is created from these theories. The active search for a problem or disease (clearly based on the premise of medicine, hence the medical model) proceeds, in part, from the assertions that there exists

---

Note to the Trainer

The background material outlined in the discussion section is provided to better prepare you for possible participant questions. The information given here should not be presented in its entirety. The material can be integrated into this and subsequent sections of the training program.

in the world concrete, definable, and hopefully available solutions to the identified problem. Such linear thinking ignores the uncertainty and complexity that characterizes the human condition and human relationships.

2. The strengths model is very different from prevailing long-term care models. For example, the model is oriented toward assessing and building on the strengths of individuals, groups, and communities. A person's needs are not ignored; instead, strengths are used to guide the selection and course of the endeavors to successfully resolve the stated problems.

3. Traditional medical-rehabilitative models tend to focus on physical or mental impairments and offer solutions through prescribing and delivering services. Authority is placed in professional decision making. The desired outcome is maximum body function as determined by medical standards. The strengths model focuses on attaining clients' goals and views clients as being in charge of caregiving.

4. Medical-rehabilitative models have a valid role when acute medical needs precipitate hospitalization and rehabilitation in a skilled nursing facility. For the most part, however, older people with a disability and/or ongoing illnesses are not acutely ill. Episodic hospitalizations occur, but their overall needs relate to many aspects of daily living that require the use of a broad range of services and resources.

5. Aging is stigmatizing in American society. People generalize about older people and discriminate against them based on negative stereotypes. An older person's sense of control can be challenged by, for example, negative images in the media or by a peer group whose members are less physically impaired than he or she. Continually confronted with images of dependence, many older adults readily accept cultural definitions of what it is to be old, especially those that are dictated by professional caregivers.

6. The strengths model recognizes that, in isolation, medical models are inadequate to deal with the largely social and personal care needs of older people. Consider the case of an older person who is confined to a wheelchair but does not have an acute illness. This person may be given any number of diagnoses, with a possible professional directive for placement in institutional care, even though the primary barrier to living at home is physical access. By using the strategies outlined in the strengths model, the care manager would obtain a holistic picture of the person's needs, of which only one is medical care, and would explore all available options for meeting these needs.

7. The "Models of Helping" handout demonstrates the dramatic differences in orientation among the strengths model and the medical-rehabilitation models. Typically, within the medical models the focus is on diagnosing and treating a specific ailment

rather than evaluating and addressing the well-being of the whole person. For example, a person with a broken hip might be hospitalized, treated, and released. The person's medical needs may have been met, but matters such as personal mobility, independent living skills, and other social factors may never be weighed (Smith & Eggleston, 1989).

Strengths Care Management Functions

Learning Unit 6

Purpose:

To provide participants with an understanding of the care management functions of the strengths model

Approximate Time Required:

30 minutes

Supplies:

Make photocopies of the handout "Steps in the Helping Journey" and the flow chart "The Strengths Model of Care Management" (see pp. 20 and 21)

Instructions:

1. Review the six service system functions, which are found in the discussion points that follow and in the handout "Steps in the Helping Journey." The functions should be introduced to participants by distributing this handout and photocopies of the flow chart "The Strengths Model of Care Management." You may want to make overhead transparencies of these two tools so that participants can follow along easily during the discussion. It is not important to describe each function in detail and with specificity.

2. Describe to participants how the six care management functions represent the flow of care management. Emphasize that care management is *rarely ever* a linear process, despite what the diagram represents. For example, an activity that occurs during engagement such as information gathering also may appear during the strengths inventory and personal goal-planning phases. Another example is when only short-term resource acquisition is needed, and the client–care manager work will proceed rapidly from engagement to implementation to graduated disengagement. Both instances depict the ways in which the functions are not rigidly defined steps.

3. You can give case examples to illustrate each of the six phases of the care management process. Inherent in each phase are a number of essential care management roles and activities performed by the care manager and the client. Reassure participants that they will have a better grasp of these functions as training progresses. Future modules will focus on each of the key functions.

Discussion Points:

1. Engagement
   - Initial contacts and meetings between client and care manager
   - Unstructured, conversational approach rather than a rigid, formal interview process
   - Exploration of common interests and experiences to build rapport
   - Purpose of care management and mutual expectations are discussed by both parties
   - Client's concerns and interests are validated and accepted

2. Strengths Inventory
   - Past and present individual and environmental strengths, abilities, and accomplishments are gathered across six areas of daily living, including physical, social, and emotional well-being.
   - Viewed as an ongoing process that is generated by both client and care manager
   - Client identifies priorities from his or her wants, which are used as a basis for goal development
   - Client's interests, wants, and needs are recorded in each life domain
   - Past and present attempts to use community resources are recorded in each life domain.
   - Information is gathered conversationally and, ideally, is introduced after a certain degree of trust has been established.

3. Personal Goal Planning
   - Focuses on achieving client-set goals through a collaboratively developed plan of action
   - Client's priority wants and needs taken from the strengths inventory form the basis for goal development
   - Long-term goals are broken down into a series of short-term tasks.
   - Specifies responsibilities and target dates for the tasks
   - Client's personal and environmental resources, naturally occurring helpers, and services are identified to assist in implementing goals

4. Resource Acquisition
   - Obtain environmental resources and services desired by clients to achieve their goals

- Ensure that community resources and services are available, accessible, accommodating, and adequate to meet client needs and preferences
- Negotiate with service providers and naturally occurring helpers on behalf of client's rights
- Use assertive outreach to natural helpers and naturally occurring resources
- Creative integration of client's personal and environmental strengths into the desired goals

5. Continuing Collaboration
- Typically thought of as monitoring
- Tasks listed on the personal plan are carried out
- Frequent and continuous communication with a collective of paid and unpaid helpers
- Naturally occurring helpers and caregivers receive ongoing direction, praise, and feedback
- Meetings are held to resolve conflicts, and helping efforts are regularly reevaluated

6. Graduated Disengagement
- Natural interdependence is promoted by creating opportunities for increasing client reliance on sustainable support networks
- Clients are contacted less frequently, but they are reassured of available support if circumstances change
- Number and variety of naturally occurring helpers and resources are increased to phase out the need for care management services

Defining Strengths

When talking to clients; writing assessments, care plans,
and progress notes; or discussing your clients with others, always consider their

Knowledge, learning, and self-awareness

Achievements

Talents and hobbies

Individual characteristics

Pride, dignity, and self-image

Choices and desires

Families and social relationships

Coping mechanisms

Experiences

Feelings and emotions

Cultural values, customs, and traditions

Participation in community and creative activities

Willingness to ask for and receive help

Physical, mental, and functional status

External resources or access to basic life necessities

Values

Strengths-Based Care Management for Older Adults. © 2000, Health Professions Press, Inc.

Self-Assessment Guide

The assessment process should begin with the client's view of the situation.

Agree———————————————————————————————Disagree

Older adults have identifiable strengths.

Agree———————————————————————————————Disagree

A trusting relationship is key to effective care management practice.

Agree———————————————————————————————Disagree

Building on clients' strengths fosters their motivation to change.

Agree———————————————————————————————Disagree

All older people have the capacity to learn, grow, and change.

Agree———————————————————————————————Disagree

Every environment is full of resources.

Agree———————————————————————————————Disagree

If the care manager is concerned for a client's health and/or safety, the care manager has the right to override the client's wishes.

Agree———————————————————————————————Disagree

Strengths-Based Care Management for Older Adults © 2000, Health Professions Press, Inc.

Strengths Model Principles

Discovering and building on strengths rather than problems facilitates hope and self-reliance.

Older people have the power to learn, grow, and change.

Relationship building is essential to effective efforts to help clients.

Older people can participate in decisions, make choices, and determine the direction of the helping process.

Resource acquisition includes assertive outreach to all community resources.

Strengths-Based Care Management for Older Adults. © 2000, Health Professions Press, Inc.

Models of Helping

Traditional models

Social role	Taking care of elders
Who controls the helping process?	Professional authority and control
Solution to problems	Professional-oriented assessment and service delivery
Care management relationship	Clients are passive receptacles for agency-directed interventions
Services and supports	Prescribed levels of service

Strengths model

	Elders taking care of themselves
	Consumer authority and control
	Determined by the consumer and the environment
	Clients are active partners who direct the helping process
	Services and supports are customized to meet the client's needs, not the provider's

Strengths-Based Care Management for Older Adults. © 2000, Health Professions Press, Inc.

Strengths Model versus Medical Models of Practice

	Strengths model	Medical-rehabilitative models of practice
Value base for helping efforts	Clients have the potential to grow, heal, and learn Clients have the ability to identify their own wants and needs Human individuality, uniqueness	Problem resolution depends on professional expertise Clients lack insight and knowledge about themselves and their problems
Solution to problems	Within clients and their environments Naturally occurring community resources used first	Professional-oriented assessment and service delivery Compliance with prescribed treatments and clinical pathways
Care management relationship	Client-directed decision making Emphasis on developing rapport and trust Care manager replaces self when possible with naturally occurring helpers	Provider-directed decision making and interventions Relationship depends on professional knowledge to determine the specific nature of the problem
Care management tasks	Assisting clients with personal goal achievement Rejuvenating and creating naturally occurring helping networks Providing services within the context of the person's needs and wants	Teaching skills to overcome deficits Monitoring compliance Medical management of identified problems
Desired client outcomes	Interdependence Increased quality of life Self-efficacy Client satisfaction	Problem resolution Maximum body function Meeting identified biomedical standards of treatment

Steps in the Helping Journey

Engagement

Initial contacts
Informal and conversational
Explore common interests/experiences
Delineate mutual expectations
Validate/accept client concerns

Strengths Inventory

Collect information on personal/environmental strengths
Viewed as ongoing process
Client identifies priorities
Record interests, wants, needs in life domains
Record past, present community resources
Present information to client

Personal Goal Planning

Focus on achieving client-set goals through a collaboratively developed plan of action
Priority wants and needs form basis for goal development
Identify goals and divide into tasks
Specify responsibility and target dates for tasks
Identify resources, helpers, services

Resource Acquisition

Access resources and services to achieve goals
Ensure community resources, services are appropriate
Negotiate with service and resource providers
Provide assertive outreach to naturally occurring helpers and resources
Integrate strengths, resources into goals

Continuing Collaboration

Perceived as monitoring
Carry out tasks
Sustain client gains
Frequent, continuous contact
Provide ongoing direction, praise, feedback to caregivers
Resolve conflicts/reevaluate process regularly

Graduated Disengagement

Contacts become less frequent
Reassure client of continued support if needed
Replace formal services with naturally occurring helpers

Strengths-Based Care Management for Older Adults. © 2000, Health Professions Press, Inc.

The Strengths Model of Care Management Flow Chart

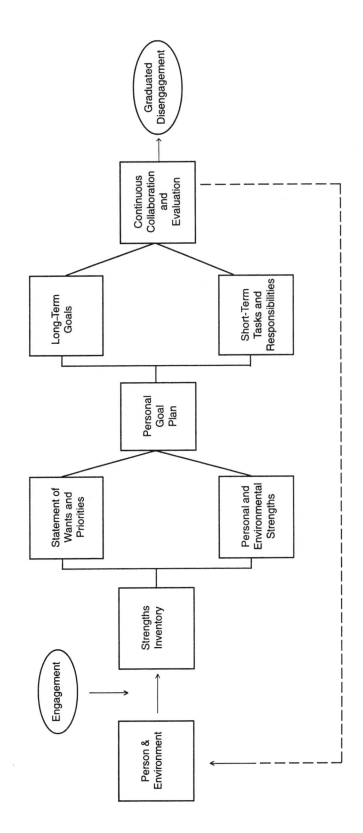

Module 2

Engagement
Establishing the Helping Relationship

Engagement is the process of building relationships with clients and is the initial phase of assessment. At this stage the primary objective for the care manager and client is to get to know each other better. This does not mean that you will become friendly with every client. Care managers should acknowledge that clients enter into the relationship hoping to improve their life situations. You may become one of an older client's most important relationships. Therefore, the client–care manager relationship should be treated seriously. During the initial meetings with a client, the care manager does not presume to hold the answers to the client's problems but rather assists him or her in developing the skills needed to resolve the situation.

An effective working relationship results simply from spending time nurturing the relationship. Find out about your clients. What do they like to do? How do they spend their time? Caring in this context means that clients believe that actions taken on their part will be in their best interest and are something that they want.

Often, changes are achieved because of the client's faith in the care manager's judgment. The client attempts to take more responsibility for his or her life solely because the care manager believes that it can be done. In this way, the strength of the relationship becomes a vehicle to help the client bring about the needed changes.

In the strengths model engagement includes the following components:

- An open, conversational approach rather than a rigid, formal interview process
- An atmosphere that is characterized by warmth, genuineness, open communication, and appropriate levels of self-disclosure
- Time spent getting to know each other as people by seeking areas of common interest
- A delineation of roles and mutual expectations among professionals, clients, and caregiver

Successful engagement is accomplished by maintaining regular and frequent contact during the initial weeks of contact. If the client is not comfortable with regular face-to-face contact, then indirect interactions such as letters, notes, and telephone calls can foster trust and precipitate the relationship-development process. The care manager demonstrates commitment to the relationship by maintaining personal contact during illnesses and less-frequent contact during periods that require less interaction (Rapp, 1998).

The client's interests, desires, and abilities should guide the engagement process. Care managers can help build the relationship by (Kisthardt & Rapp, 1992)

- Educating the person about how involvement with the care manager can help him or her realize what he or she wants in life
- Asking the client and his or her primary caregiver how they view the care manager and what they expect from the relationship
- Accepting the client's definition of the issues to be addressed
- Identifying and building on existing strengths
- Assuming that establishing a positive helping relationship with the person is of the utmost importance to a successful working relationship
- Giving lots of positive feedback, celebrating accomplishments, and exhibiting continuing interest in the client

Recognizing Commonalities[1]

Purpose:

To help participants understand the importance of developing trust and rapport during the initial meetings with clients

Approximate Time Required:

45 minutes

Supplies:

Make an overhead transparency and photocopies of the handout "Steps to Fostering an Effective Working Relationship" (see p. 34); overhead projector and marker

Instructions:

1. Ask trainees to find a partner (preferably someone who is not sitting next to him or her). After partners have been chosen, ask the pairs to identify what they have in com-

---

[1]Learning Unit 8 can be used as a supplement to this unit or may be substituted for this activity.

mon; for example, hair color, children, hobbies, credit card debt, and so forth. Allow 10 minutes for this exchange.

2. After 10 minutes, bring the groups together to discuss what they found out about one another. Highlight the commonalities that exist within and between the different small groups. Ask participants if any of them were not able to find something in common. The participants will indicate through nodding their heads that they were able to connect with their partner. After looking around the room for positive nonverbal expressions, stress how the entire group was able to find something in common with their partners.

3. After several people have discussed their findings, ask participants questions from a typical functional assessment. The following questions usually precipitate laughter from the group:
   - Did anyone ask his or her partner about his or her bowel movements?
   - Did anyone ask his or her partner if he or she is incontinent?
   - How many of you used the following mental status exam items with your partner? Name the president of the United States. I want you to remember the following three words: pencil, apple, bed. In a few minutes I will ask you to repeat the three words. Toileting questions also are classic examples for examining people's mental status: "Have you ever had a client wearing incontinence pads tell you that he or she does not have problems with incontinence?" A client's answer can be assessed as uncooperative, confusion, a lie, or preservation of pride and dignity.

4. Discuss how such questions can be humiliating for an older person and possibly damage his or her self-esteem.

5. Discuss the importance of first meetings, how new relationships are normally established, and how different the typical process is from traditional in-home assessment interviewing. The following questions can be used to facilitate the discussion:
   - Did my questions on bowel movements and continence feel rather intrusive? Why?
   - Are there ways to gather information in a less intrusive manner?
   - How many of you felt as though you were being interviewed? Was the tone conversational?
   - Were any of you embarrassed by the questions?
   - How many of you self-disclosed?
   - Did anyone write down what his or her partner said?
   - How many of you laughed?
   - Did you learn anything that you could write in the person's assessment?

6. Conclude the discussion by distributing the handout "Steps to Fostering an Effective Working Relationship" to participants and presenting it as an overhead transparency.

The discussion points listed here can be integrated into the discussion of the steps. Summarize the discussion by emphasizing how different their process of getting to know their partner was from a traditional assessment interview. In addition, stress how much they learned about the other person in just 5–10 minutes.

Discussion Points:

1. The engagement process is viewed as a distinct activity that constitutes the initial step in developing the client–care manager relationship.

2. The time that you spend during the beginning stages to develop rapport can make or break the subsequent assessment and planning phases. If your client feels more comfortable with you, he or she will speak more openly with you. Spending time developing rapport can facilitate the interview process, you will gather more valuable information, and you will have more fun.

3. If you have developed rapport and trust with your client, you will not feel as embarrassed asking difficult questions, such as those regarding toileting. In addition, your client will have a better understanding of the importance of collecting information and will not feel as uncomfortable talking about, for example, incontinence or financial status.

4. Whenever we meet someone new, we form impressions of the person. Your clients also are making judgments about you. In essence, your clients are interviewing you. They are asking themselves why you are helping them and what you want from them. Your clients may be thinking, "What should I tell her?" "Should I tell her about my heating bill?" "Should I let him know that I'm really not able to take a full bath, only sponge baths?" "If I tell her, will she put me in a nursing home?"

5. As care managers, we need to learn and know what our clients have done, how they have done it, what they have learned from doing it, who was involved in doing it, and what resources (internal and external) were available as they overcame their problems.

6. The optimal climate for care management services begins during the very first contact with the client. The climate must be one that engenders productive communication and relationship skills. During the engagement stage, the care manager seeks to develop trust by conveying concern and capability. He or she does this by using reflective listening, which demonstrates an attitude of thoughtful concern, and by providing concrete services, such as getting Meals on Wheels initiated or the client's heating bill taken care of. These actions signal to the client that the case manager is capable, competent, and reliable.

7. An in-home assessment of an older adult requires the care manager to come equipped with good communication skills, including listening, questioning, paraphrasing, clarifying, and summarizing. Skillful care managers have learned the art of listening, questioning, and responding to obtain information, establish rapport, develop a relationship, and promote client understanding. In addition, there are many special issues and concerns that often must be addressed when communicating with older adults, such as hearing and visual limitations, language impairments, and decline in mental functioning.

Implementing the Engagement Process

Learning Unit 8

Purpose:
To facilitate participants' understanding of engagement skills and first-meeting interactions; this activity can be used instead of the "Recognizing Commonalities" exercise (Learning Unit 7) or as a supplement to it.

Approximate Time Required:
30 minutes

Supplies:
Markers, flipchart; make photocopies of the handout "Questions for Successful First Meetings" (see p. 35)

Instructions:
1. Ask for two volunteers to conduct an interview in front of the group. One of the volunteers will assume the role of care manager and the other will take the role of a client.
2. Explain to the care manager that he or she has 10 minutes to get to know his or her client.
3. Ask for two volunteers who have good handwriting. Give each person a marker. Ask one of the volunteers to record the care manager's questions on the flipchart and the other person to record the client's responses.
4. Have the interviewee and the interviewer give feedback to each other and to the group about how they experienced the questions. Ask them to identify any nonver-

bal clues they noticed that were given by the other party. Encourage them to share whether they felt respected and how comfortable the experience was for them.

5. Ask the group to indicate what actions they saw as helpful to fostering a working relationship. For example, did both parties share information? How much self-disclosure evolved between the two parties? Did the group find the interview to be a directed, unstructured, professional conversation? How did the stated interview questions provide a useful starting point to begin the helping relationship?

6. Review the questions that have been listed on the flipchart. Highlight the questions asked by the interviewer that also are listed in the handout "Questions for Successful First Meetings."

Relationships and Grape Juice

Learning Unit 9

Purpose:

To further participant knowledge about establishing and developing relationships

Approximate Time Required:

45 minutes

Supplies:

5 × 8 inch blank index cards, pens or pencils, flipchart and marker, empty frozen grape juice can (if readily available)

Instructions:

1. Distribute the index cards. Draw a picture of a can of grape juice on the flipchart or display an empty frozen grape juice container. Say to the group, "This is a can of frozen grape juice. I would like you to pretend that you are a can of frozen grape juice. Now, write down on your card how you would like to be opened." Allow about 3 minutes for participants to write their responses.

2. Go around the room and ask participants to elaborate on their responses. Record key words on a board or flipchart. Do not discuss or interpret responses at this time. Once all of the participants have responded, facilitate the discussion by asking the following questions:

    • "Anything else on how you should be opened?"

- •"Who should open you?"
- •"What could be some of the reasons for not opening you?"
- •"What should we do with you once you are opened?"

Possible participant responses include

- •"Open me slowly, carefully, and gently so you won't hurt me."
- •"Use the electric can opener. It's faster and cleaner and won't hurt as much."
- •"Don't use a can opener. It'll cut me."
- •"Thaw me out first. Let me sit on the counter for a while to warm up so I'll pour out better."
- •"Don't dig me out with a spoon when I'm still frozen."
- •"Dispose of me properly. I don't want to be kicked around the alley."
- •"I'd rather not be opened at all."

3. When participants run out of responses, start a discussion of how the activity corresponds to issues of intimacy that arise during the engagement stage. For example
   - •The client's ambivalence about getting involved with the care manager
   - •The care manager's ambivalence about getting too emotionally involved with the client
   - •The working relationship's forced intimacy

   Ask participants, "What is your style of intimacy?" "How do you facilitate trust and intimacy so that your client doesn't feel like a grape juice can that was opened, contents poured out, and tossed in the trash?" Possible responses include

   - •Healthy intimacy usually develops over a period of time.
   - •The benefits of intimacy include feeling accepted and cared for, honesty, and mutual trust.
   - •The more intimate we are with others, the more vulnerable we feel and the more easily others can hurt us.
   - •Relationships that are built on trust, acceptance, and mutual appreciation foster the development of a healthy client–care manager working partnership.

4. Define behavioral indicators of trust. Elicit from the group their definitions of trust and how they would describe a trusting relationship. Record participant responses on a flipchart or overhead. After compiling at least 10 indicators of trust (e.g., honesty, caring, sincerity, "being real," following through, active listening, share decision making), summarize the importance of demonstrating these core qualities in one's care management practice. Call the group's attention to how difficult trust is for many clients to feel because it involves risking themselves by sharing their thoughts, feelings, weaknesses, and failures with their care manager.

5. Conclude the discussion by asking participants to think about their experiences as a care recipient and a caregiver. What made the relationship feel good or helpful? Integrate the following points into the discussion:
   - Care managers need to allow the trust process to develop naturally and at the client's pace rather than forcing the issue by saying things like, "You can trust me!"
   - Care managers must demonstrate that they can be trusted by keeping their promises, following through on tasks, and maintaining regular contact.

Obstacles to Engagement

Learning Unit 10

Purpose:
To identify strategies for dealing with clients who resist engaging with their care manager

Approximate Time Required:
45 minutes

Supplies:
Notepads or paper and pencils or pens; flipchart and marker; make photocopies of the handout "Obstacles to Engagement" (see p. 36)

Instructions:
1. Ask each participant to find a partner. Distribute the handout "Obstacles to Engagement."
2. Ask the partners to discuss the obstacles that are outlined in the handout and to jot down possible strategies to address each of the obstacles. Allow about 15 minutes for partners to meet.
3. Reconvene the large group. Facilitate a discussion of each obstacle by asking participant groups to share possible solutions to each problem. Typically, groups generate an abundance of ideas and solutions.
4. Record participant answers on the flipchart or overhead.
5. Facilitate a discussion on participants' understanding of resistance to the helping relationship. Care managers often use the word "resistant" to describe a client's unwillingness to participate fully in the helping process.

6. Ask participants to list other ways (apart from what was listed on the handout) in which resistance is manifested during the engagement process. Possible responses include
    •Being verbally hostile
    •Saying one thing and doing another
    •Denying their need for help
7. Validate the group for identifying numerous productive approaches to dealing with resistance. Ask the participants to share any other ways they have handled client resistance in the past.
8. Discuss the importance of perceiving resistance or reluctance to engagement as normal, particularly in the early stages of a helping relationship. Understanding and accepting the obstacles to engagement is a necessary first step in engaging the older person in a helping relationship. Care managers must try continually to understand the reasons for resistance so that they can identify productive approaches for responding to the situation.

Listen to a Client for a Change

> **Learning Unit 11**

Purpose:
To help participants understand the engagement process from the client's point of view

Approximate Time Required:
60 minutes

Supplies:
Make photocopies of the handout "Interview Questions to Get the Client's Perspective" (see p. 37)

Instructions:
1. Distribute the handout "Interview Questions for the Client's Perspective." Participants ask these questions after the clients have provided some background information about themselves and their reasons for seeking care management services.
2. The discussion with the client concludes with any additional questions from the participants. Dismiss the visiting clients.

Note to the Trainer

This discussion activity creates an opportunity for two or more older people who currently receive care management services to participate in the training session. If possible, invite clients from different ethnic and racial backgrounds to increase participants' knowledge about cultural differences that can arise during engagement. Ask clients to prepare notes about their background, why they are consumers of care management services, and what they appreciate about their care managers.

---

3. After the presenters have left, discuss participants' reactions to the clients' presentations.

Discussion Points:

1. Focus the discussion on setting boundaries with clients and the differences between friendships and professional relationships. Typically, during the presentation, one or both of the recipients of care management services will refer to their care manager as their friend. It also is common for clients to define the relationship by using friendship descriptors.

2. Lead a group discussion by asking participants, "What are the differences between professional helping relationships and friendships?" Record participants' responses on a flipchart. Some possible responses follow:
   - Helping relationships have a defined purpose and role—to help clients reach their goals and live as independently as possible.
   - A helping relationship is constrained and limited by time factors.
   - The helping relationship should benefit the client more than the care manager.
   - A professional helping relationship does not include soliciting support and advice from a client.
   - The helping relationship is a planned and controlled relationship, whereas friendships develop spontaneously.
   - In a professional relationship the care manager receives more information than the client does, and the balance of power is unequal.

3. Continue the discussion by asking, "How much self-disclosure is appropriate?" Some possible responses follow:
   - Appropriate levels of self-disclosure are important to developing relationships and to establishing trust, as long as disclosure is used purposively with clients.
   - The purpose of self-disclosure in helping relationships is to meet the needs of clients, not the care manager's.

•The amount and degree of disclosure that is comfortable and appropriate is different for each care manager.

4. Conclude the learning unit by emphasizing that care managers are not "paid friends." The relationship is indeed friendly because it involves warmth, acceptance, and respect, but it is not a friendship. Clients need to understand that their relationship with their care manager is time limited, so the care manager should devote considerable effort to help the person build real friendships with other people.

Steps to Fostering an Effective Working Relationship

The basic elements of the engagement process include the following:

- Contacting the client on a regular and frequent basis during the beginning stages

- Spending time getting to know each other by identifying common interests

- Educating the client on the ways in which the care management relationship is beneficial

- Accepting the client's definition of the issues to be addressed

- Delineating roles and mutual expectations among professionals, clients, and caregivers

During the engagement process, the care manager

- Uses an open, conversational approach rather than a rigid, formal interview process

- Demonstrates interest in the client and his or her view of the situation

- Moves at the client's pace

- Uses appropriate levels of self-disclosure

- Does not assume the client will know what care management services are or will want help

- Has no preconceived plan

- Creates a climate with lots of positive feedback and validation

Strengths-Based Care Management for Older Adults. © 2000, Health Professions Press, Inc.

Questions for Successful First Meetings

Have you lived in this area a long time? Where are you originally from? Where have you lived most of your life?

How many children (grandchildren, great grandchildren) do you have? Do they live around here? Do you get to see them often?

Is religion a part of your life? Are you active in your church or synagogue?

Are you a member of any clubs or groups? What have you liked best about being a member?

How much schooling do you have? Did you attend college? What are your memories of school?

What kind(s) of work have you done or do you still do? How did you spend your time when you weren't working?

What do you enjoy doing in your leisure time? How do you like to spend your day?

Do you read? What do you like to read?

Do you like movies? Television? What are your favorite movies? What are your favorite programs?

Were you ever (are you now) interested in sports? If so, in which sports did (do) you participate? Do you enjoy being a spectator? What are your favorite sports/teams? Do you have any favorite athletes?

What kinds of music do you like? Did you ever (do you) play an instrument or sing?

Strengths-Based Care Management for Older Adults. © 2000, Health Professions Press, Inc.

Obstacles to Engagement

Obstacles (emotions or behaviors) to establishing relationships with clients	Suggested care manager response
Suspicion of care manager	
Saying "no" prematurely to the initial meeting or subsequent meetings	
Not letting the care manager in the house	
Excessive anger toward the system	
Refusal to talk or respond to questions	
Communicates using racist statements and attitudes	
Not keeping the appointment or continually changing the established appointment time	

Strengths-Based Care Management for Older Adults. © 2000, Health Professions Press, Inc.

Interview Questions to Get the Client's Perspective

How would you describe your care manager?

How did you feel as you anticipated your first meeting with your care manager?

What did your care manager do that helped you during your first meeting?

After the initial contact, what did your care manager do that worked for you?

What did he or she do that didn't work for you?

What piece of advice would you give to your care manager?

What was it about your relationship with your care manager that you appreciated most?

Assessment from a Strengths Approach

Assessment from a strengths perspective is a holistic rather than a diagnostic process. By helping clients to feel a sense of control and competence, a care manager enhances their sense of competence and ability to achieve goals. It is an act of injustice and oppression against a client to suppose that the whole picture of this person is captured in a diagnostic, functional, or psychotherapeutic assessment.

Naming illnesses and problems alone, as in the case of functional assessments, does not provide a complete or accurate picture of an older person's strengths, coping capacities, motivations, and potential for change. Using the strengths approach, the focus is no longer simply on the client's problems but on his or her successes as well (DeJong & Miller, 1995). This change of focus means accounting for what an older person wants, is doing, and can do to maintain his or her independence. In supporting a client's strengths, a care manager projects an honest belief in the client's ability to deal with his or her problems.

Maluccio (1981) found that care managers tend to ignore or underestimate client strengths by focusing solely on the individual's problems and deficits, which ultimately impairs his or her ability to discern the potential for growth, reinforce self-confidence and self-respect, and discontinue services when they are no longer needed.

Most care managers are committed to acknowledging their clients' strengths. However, the majority of assessment and care planning tools allow only minimal space for recording strengths, hindering even the best intentions. Rarely, if ever, are client strengths perceived as integral to care planning in such a way that services are provided and activities are structured to maximize and promote existing or potential strengths (Kivnick, 1993). Services are allocated based on what is essential to maintain or increase, not weaken, an older person's sense of him- or herself. Subsequently, care managers fall back easily into old habits and become preoccupied with a client's diagnosis and problems. The strengths inventory is a mechanism for facilitating a care manager's commitment to client strengths, resources, and potential.

Most of all, assessment from a strengths perspective affirms and respects an older person's dignity and self-worth.

Benefits of Using a Strengths Assessment

The strengths approach to assessment assists the care manager in getting to know an older person in a holistic way, which creates a positive interaction and builds rapport. Developing and nurturing the client–care manager relationship facilitates the care manager's ability to tap into the individual's unique characteristics and life experiences to prevent unwanted or unnecessary formal services. The established relationship allows the care manager, using the strengths inventory, to identify what successes can be drawn on for care planning, with careful attention given to not replace successful efforts by informal caregivers. Furthermore, the strengths model's services and resources are used based on what the client wants, not on the current menu of reimbursable services.

Reduction in care management costs and paid services can be attributed to assessment methods that focus on crafting a plan of action based on client knowledge and motivation rather than on professional knowledge of diseases and functional limitations alone. These assessment processes also reduce costs by emphasizing the use of naturally occurring resources. The structure and the format of the inventory encourages care managers to assertively pursue and find available environmental and community resources rather than calling on formal service providers to fill the void in the person's support network (Fast & Chapin, 1996).

The Strengths Inventory

The purpose of conducting a strengths inventory is to capitalize on strengths that the client relies on or has relied on to resolve current issues and meet needs. The strengths inventory gathers information that focuses on a person's personal and environmental strengths from six interrelated categories or life domains: daily living situation, health, finances/insurance, social supports, leisure/recreational interests, and spirituality/religion. The strengths inventory is a systematic strategy for identifying strengths and using them to help clients reach their goals.

The strengths inventory gathers information regarding an older person's current situation, wants and needs for the future, and past achievements, using the framework of the six life domains. The first three life domains relate to basic survival needs; the last three address a meaningful quality of life. The strengths inventory was developed and based on the assumption that an individual's behavior is influenced by his or her life history, present social context, and needs. Identifying information within each life domain directs and supports the short-term goals that were developed during the personal goal-planning stage.

The strengths inventory helps the care manager enter the client's world by looking for the presence of personal and environmental resources rather than the absence of skills, abilities, supports, and so forth. The central tenet is not what kind of life one *has* but what kind of life one *wants* by bringing together the resources needed to satisfy these wants. Together, the older person and the care manager seek to discover the individual and community resources on which the client can draw and to identify the client's priorities or sense of urgency for care planning across the various life domains.

It is not always possible to replace existing standardized functional and/or eligibility assessments with the strengths inventory. Rules and regulations established by many public funding sources for conferring benefits and allocating care often stipulate that the services rendered depend on the type and number of problems or disabilities. However, the value of the strengths assessment process is not lost when it is used to "supplement rather than to supplant existing assessments" (Kisthardt, 1992, p. 69).

Strengths Assessment Fundamentals

| Learning Unit 12 |

Purpose:
To help participants understand how the strengths assessment process differs from the use of a functional assessment as the basis for personal goal planning

Approximate Time Required:
60 minutes

Supplies:
Make photocopies of the "Sam" and "Elaine" case studies and both case study questions (see pp. 47 and 48)

Instructions:
1. Engagement is separated from assessment in the strengths model because of the importance of establishing rapport with clients during initial contacts. However, the two functions are not always distinct steps. The engagement information often becomes the starting point for the assessment phase and subsequently, the two functions become intertwined. Explain to the group that you would like them to have a better understanding of a strengths-based assessment process before they start using the strengths inventory tool. Introduce the following activity and the rationale for using a case study format.
2. Divide the group into two sections. Distribute copies of the two case studies, "Sam" and "Elaine," to both sections. Ask participants to read Sam and Elaine's case studies and record their answers in the space provided under each question. Allow 15–20 minutes for this part of the exercise. Inevitably, after reading the case studies, some of

---

Note to the Trainer

Services should be allocated based on an assessment that maintains, not weakens, the older adult's sense of him- or herself. It is your ethical duty to "do no harm" and to not make the person feel terrible after the interview. Only by creating *life plans* rather than *care plans* will an older person be able to live meaningfully.

---

the participants will ask for more information. Instead of giving them more information, you can enhance the learning process by asking participants to write down their questions and discuss their relevance at an appropriate point.

3. Display the case study questions on an overhead transparency or write them on a chalkboard. Ask each section of the group to discuss their answers with the full group. (The fourth question will likely generate the most diverse answers.)

4. As the sections share their answers, guide the group in integrating "Sam's" or "Elaine's" identified strengths with ideas for addressing the outlined concerns, needs, and wants. If participants complain that both "Elaine" and "Sam" fail to specify what they want to change in their lives, ask the group to discern possible clues from their case situations.

5. Conclude the exercise by explaining how each group demonstrated the ability to address "Sam's" and "Elaine's" needs by using his or her strengths as an intervention tool. If applicable, identify any responses that are listed under professional areas of concern, which also were addressed by using strengths-based strategies. Congratulate the participants on their ability to organize and integrate critical assessment information without using a structured, systematic assessment tool. Summarize the exercise's purpose by emphasizing that, in essence, they conducted a basic strengths assessment.

Conducting a Strengths Inventory

Learning Unit 13

Purpose:
To help participants master the knowledge and skills needed to conduct a strengths inventory

Approximate Time Required:
120 minutes (2 hours)

Supplies:

Make photocopies of the handouts "Strengths Inventory (Sample)" (you need to make two copies for each participant), "Ann's Strengths Inventory" (also make overhead transparencies of the sample inventory and Ann's inventory), "Conducting the Strengths Inventory," "Sample Questions for Strengths Inventory Discussions," and "Essential Components of a Strengths Inventory" (see pp. 49–55); pencils or pens; overhead projector and marker; flipchart and marker

Instructions:

1. Introduce the strengths inventory by presenting a strong rationale for its utility with older adults:

    • "Life is more than a list of ADLs and IADLs." The way in which long-term care services are typically delivered predisposes care managers to view older people as a deteriorating bundle of needs. People's needs are categorized using standardized assessments in terms of activities of daily living (ADLs) and instrumental activities of daily living (IADLs). Because of the amount of emphasis placed on ADLs and IADLs, service providers tend to conceptualize the meaning of life as revolving around the number of ADLs that older people perform. Sadly, older adults soon realize that to receive help, they also must perceive themselves in these terms.

    • A strengths-based assessment strives to preserve older people's dignity and self-respect. The consequences of the assessment process can be enormous for older adults. Standardized functional or medical assessments often force them to come to grips with a loss of function when, in fact, they perceive themselves as independent. The strengths inventory is geared toward not reducing the reality of older adults' lives—their wishes, beliefs, histories, likes, and dislikes—to a list of problems.

2. Display the overhead transparency of the sample strengths inventory and ask the participants to follow along with you on their handouts. Discuss the format and structure of the strengths inventory. Explain how the strengths inventory is divided into three columns and six rows. The strengths inventory gathers information regarding an older person's current situation and wants and needs for the future in the first two columns and information about past achievements in the third column, using the framework of the six life domains. The first three life domains (daily living situation, health, and finances/insurance) relate to basic survival needs; the latter three (social supports, spirituality/religion, and leisure/recreational interests) address a meaningful quality of life.

3. Display the overhead transparency "Ann's Strengths Inventory" and ask participants to follow along with you on their handouts. Use this inventory to describe to the group how information is gathered from a person's past, current situation, and future wants within each of the following domains:

   •**Daily living situation**—focuses on home environment, transportation, whether the person lives alone, and whether he or she has access to basic material needs, such as laundry and shopping

   •**Physical/emotional health**—involves the status of a person's physical and emotional health and the resources that are needed to maintain or promote physical and emotional health, including diet, medications, and equipment

   •**Finances/insurance**—pertains to the sources and amount of income, private insurance plans, as well as universal benefits such as Medicare and Social Security

   •**Social supports**—includes family, neighbors, pets, church, and other social contacts (e.g., hairdresser, coffee shop waitress, other helpers that an individual sees daily) that give meaning to the individual's life; present this domain to participants as encompassing people, activities, animals, and material things

   •**Spirituality/religion**—focuses on the role and relevance of faith, spirituality, and formal religion in the person's life

   •**Leisure/recreational interests**—targets the activities, interests, and hobbies that bring enjoyment and fun to the person's life

4. Draw arrows on the overhead sample inventory to demonstrate how the interview can move from one domain to another depending on how the client responds to the care manager's questions. Stress the importance of initiating the assessment process by asking the client to select a life domain. For example, if a client expresses how he used to love to play golf, the care manager would fill out a portion of the leisure activities domain. If the client then states that he quit playing golf because of his fear of falling, then the care manager would move up to the health domain because the client shifted the discussion's focus.

5. Write on the overhead or the flipchart "Do not obsess over the cell in which to place a piece of information." Remind participants that what is important is to place the information somewhere; there is no right or wrong place to record the information. If in doubt, ask the client in which domain he or she would like the information to be placed.

6. Write on the overhead or flipchart "Be specific and descriptive." Inform participants of the importance of recording the client's answers in specific and descriptive narra-

tive terms. If the person states that he or she loves to play bridge, the recorded information also should include with whom and how often. In addition, participants should understand the ongoing nature of the strengths inventory. A client's information should always be updated and revised.

7. Use the handout "Conducting the Strengths Inventory" to present the guidelines for completing a strengths inventory. Review the handout "Sample Questions for Strengths Inventory Discussions" with participants.

8. After reviewing "Conducting the Strengths Inventory," instruct group members to find the partner with whom they met during the engagement exercise (Learning Unit 6). Distribute the second copy of the handout "Strengths Inventory (Sample)." Ask each person in the pair to interview the other person and to record his or her strengths on the blank strengths inventory form. This exercise works best if each individual in the pair represents him- or herself. Role playing the part of a care manager or a client tends to hinder the flow of communication between the two parties.

9. After the pairs have completed their inventories, bring the large group together and ask group members how they experienced the strengths inventory interview. The following are two possible questions to ask the group:
    •"What do you like or dislike about the strengths inventory?"
    •"How is this approach different from other assessment instruments that you have used?"

10. After participants share their thoughts and feelings, expand on and integrate the following into the course of the discussion:
    •You will notice that the strengths approach does not use typical phrases such as "needs to be medication compliant" or "needs to increase social skills and socialization," whereas traditional assessments skip the motivational piece—the client's wants and needs—entirely.
    •The strengths inventory uses the client's language.
    •The strengths inventory is a joint activity.
    •The client is able to tell his or her story without being confined by structured questions, and the care manager is able to flow with the information as it is being told.
    •The life domains in the strengths inventory give direction and flow to the assessment process.

11. Conclude this activity with the handout "Essential Components of a Strengths Inventory." This tool helps participants understand the importance of integrating a strengths assessment process into their daily work by using or without using a tool

like the strengths inventory. Given large caseloads, the inventory and personal planning tools can be targeted to clients at risk of nursing facility placement and individuals dealing with significant emotional and social issues, and can be introduced as an opportunity to resolve and mediate conflicts with the client's services and support systems.

"Sam"

Sam is an 80-year-old widower who moved into his 45-year-old son's house 6 months ago. He retired from his job as an accountant 8 years ago. His memory is intact, but he gets a little frustrated because it seems to take him longer than it once did to recall things. Sam's cataracts have curtailed his ability to drive.

Lately, he gets agitated easily by his three teenage grandchildren's radios, video games, and friends. Sam doesn't like taking his hypertension medications because the diuretics give him bladder control problems, which sometimes result in embarrassment. Increasingly, he doesn't want to participate in social gatherings. Sam attributes his inability to sleep at night to "not feeling well." He has lost interest in eating and says, "the food just doesn't taste good to me anymore."

Family members are frustrated that Sam refuses to participate in any hobbies or leisure activities outside the house. However, Sam does enjoy a glass or two of wine in the evening while he listens to his audio books. Family members who are at work or school until after dark are concerned that Sam is alone so much during the day.

Discussion Questions:
What are Sam's strengths?

What are Sam's losses?

As a professional involved in this case, what areas of concern emerge for you?

Using the strengths listed, identify possible options for helping Sam to address his wants and needs.

Strengths-Based Care Management for Older Adults. © 2000, Health Professions Press, Inc.

"Elaine"

Elaine is 74 years old and lives alone in a highrise retirement complex. She has three children, and none of her relatives live within driving distance. She retired from her career as an elementary school teacher 6 years ago because arthritis had impaired her mobility and her hearing was getting worse.

Her two closest female friends died in the last 6 months, and she feels overwhelmed by her loneliness and grief. Her next-door neighbor has noticed that Elaine is not eating regularly, often forgetting entirely when or whether she has eaten at all. Her neighbor says that Elaine talks often about her 10-year-old cat, visits from her grandchildren, and her quilts. Elaine's apartment is filled with children's books from her 30-year teaching career, a collection of mementos from trips around the world, and her antiques.

Elaine fears becoming totally dependent on others and being placed in a nursing facility. Because she once got her walker stuck in the elevator door, Elaine experiences feelings of panic, shortness of breath, and a smothering sensation whenever she thinks about getting in an elevator. Thus, rather than venturing out, Elaine tends to stay home, relying on her cat, reading books, and talking on the telephone with friends for comfort. She also refuses to see her physician.

Discussion Questions:

What are Elaine's strengths?

What are Elaine's losses?

As a professional involved in this case, what areas of concern emerge for you?

Using the strengths listed, identify possible options for helping Elaine to address her wants and needs.

Strengths Inventory (Sample)

Care Manager's Name _____

Client's Name _____

Current Status What do I have going for me?	Individual's Desires/Aspirations What do I want?	Personal/Social Resources What have I used in the past?
	LIFE DOMAINS	
	Daily Living Situation	
	Health	
	Finances/Insurance	
	Social Supports	
	Spirituality/Religion	
	Leisure/Recreational Interests	

continued

What Are My Priorities?

1.

2.

3.

4.

5.

Care Manager's Comments:	Client's Comments:
Care Manager's Signature Date	Client's Signature Date

Ann's Strengths Inventory

Current Status What do I have going for me?	Individual's Desires/Aspirations What do I want?	Personal/Social Resources What have I used in the past?
	LIFE DOMAINS	
75-year-old woman; lives in 1-BR apartment, nicely decorated with her own landscape paintings, maintains apartment well; doesn't drive; likes to cook; VNA is involved with home care tasks	**Daily Living Situation** "I wish I had an apartment with a second bedroom to create a painting room"; would like someone to visit with on a regular basis; is frustrated that apartment manager won't allow her to have a cat	"I had 2 hospitalizations last year: 2 weeks for breast cancer surgery and 1 month for severe depression"; "I recently moved here"; lived with daughter in San Francisco for 3 months after her husband Jim died 1 year ago
"My energy and strength fluctuates"; struggles with persistent depression, currently taking Zoloft; she smokes filtered cigarettes; her health concerns: cancer, osteoporosis, and arthritis	**Health** "I sure would like to quit the habit" (smoking); interested in finding an aqua-aerobics class; "I would like to stay out of the hospital"	"I used to meditate when I felt down"; "When Jim was alive, I was a vegetarian"; now eats out or has a frozen dinner; she and her husband used to scuba dive
Has Social Security, a small teacher's pension, a small savings account, and Medicare A and B; family helps out at times	**Finances/Insurance** Wants to increase monthly income; "I sure would like my ends to meet each month"; would like to have some money to travel	"I made good money as a teacher"; she used most of her home sale profits and savings to pay for Jim's medical expenses
Ann's brother Sam (90 years old) and her sister Rita (83 years old) live together in their parents' house several blocks away; Ann has little contact with neighbors, most of whom are much younger	**Social Supports** Wants more contact with daughter and with son, who is career Army, now living in Europe; wishes she had more friends to visit with and have fun with; "I sure miss my kids. It would be nice to see them more."	Used to have many friends; painting (watercolors) was a source of support both financially and socially through art shows; attended Methodist church prior to Jim's death; last care manager "really helped" and was "supportive"
Days are "a blur that I sometimes don't know how I am going to get through"; watches religious programs on Sunday mornings	**Spirituality/Religion** "I feel out of sorts with God, and I wish I was more connected"	"For several years I taught children's Sunday School classes"; "I don't seem to have the energy to attend much church"
Ann has watercolor supplies, but lacks a "vision of what to paint"; finds getting the supplies out too difficult at times; watches some painting shows on TV	**Leisure/Recreational Interests** Would be interested in volunteering a few hours a week at the senior center; "I would like to paint with a group of painters"; "I just want to be happy again and have some fun"	Her good friend, Dorothy, recently died from breast cancer; used to go to painter's group and art classes; called daughter a lot when Jim was alive, but phone bill got expensive; "I once read a lot, but now I end up often taking a nap."

continued

Strengths-Based Care Management for Older Adults. © 2000 Health Professions Press, Inc.

What Are My Priorities?

1. "I would like to move to a larger apartment."

2. "I want to stay out of the hospital."

3. "I just want to have fun and be happy."

4. "I want to get back into my painting again."

5.

Care Manager's Comments:	Client's Comments:
Care Manager's Signature Date	Client's Signature Date

Conducting the Strengths Inventory

- Start with the "here and now" within one life domain.
- Move to the client's expectations, hopes, and desires for that domain.
- Explore past individual and community supports that the client has used.
- Discern the individual's priorities within the various life domains.
- The strengths inventory process is never final. The process can be initiated and reinitiated.

1. Keep in mind that the strengths inventory is an ongoing process and that it is not a structured interview. Ideally, you should introduce the strengths inventory only after you have spent some time with the client.

2. Start the inventory with what you know about the client. Asking personal questions too early can violate personal boundaries. The strengths inventory can be completed over several sessions.

3. It is not essential that you fill out the entire form at the first session or even after several sessions. Follow the client's lead in what areas he or she would or would not like to discuss. Move from one life domain to another as the conversation dictates.

4. Tell your client what you're writing and ask the person if he or she would like to record any pertinent information. Use quotes from the client and language that he or she can understand.

5. Your first priority is gathering information from your client. The client is your primary source of information. The client's caregivers are a second priority.

6. You can fill out the inventory with your client or make notes after the meeting. Upon completing the life domains, review each section to make sure that your client is satisfied with the way that the information is recorded. This inventory will be constantly revised and updated throughout the helping relationship.

7. The strengths inventory concludes when you and your client prioritize the person's needs in order of importance. The identified priorities serve as a starting point for discussing personal goal attainment.

8. Both parties sign the form once it is completed. A copy of the inventory can be left with the client.

Strengths-Based Care Management for Older Adults. © 2000, Health Professions Press, Inc.

Sample Questions for Strengths Inventory Discussions

Current Status What do I have going for me?	Individual's Desires/Aspirations What do I want?	Personal/Social Resources What have I used in the past?
	LIFE DOMAINS	
What are you doing in terms of cooking meals, bathing, doing household chores, and so forth? What form(s) of transportation are you using? How secure do you feel in your home?	**Daily Living Situation** What parts of your life are important for you to stay in charge of? How satisfied are you with your current housing situation? What would make it easier for you to accept help when you wish you didn't need it?	What household chores did you enjoy or dislike? (e.g., childhood, marriage, later adult life)
How have you been feeling? What are some things you do to take care of yourself? What types of medication do you take? What are your eating habits?	**Health** What could you do to feel better? How would you like to feel?	Tell me about your health through the years—how did you handle major illnesses and injuries? What have you done in the past when you've felt down or depressed? How did you feel when you got help?
What type of insurance policies do you have? Do you receive benefits? What type? Are you able to manage financially?	**Finances/Insurance** What would give you a sense of security? What could be done to make it easier for you to continue living here?	What jobs have you held? What was your best job experience? What helped you to keep going when you went through rough times?
Tell me what a typical week is like. Who are the most important people in your life?	**Social Supports** Who would you like to see or hear from more often? Is there anything that you wish your family or friends would do for you?	Who have you turned to for support in the past? Who has turned to you for support in the past? Who has been important to you throughout your life?
How important is religion, church, or spirituality to you? What's in your life today that gives you hope?	**Spirituality/Religion** Is there anything that would make your life more satisfying?	What accomplishments are you most proud of? How have you expressed your spirituality in the past?
What activities do you enjoy? What makes you feel good?	**Leisure/Recreational Interests** Do you have any hobbies or interests that you wish you could participate in more often? Is there something you've always wanted to learn but never got around to?	When you weren't working, how did you spend your time? What did you used to enjoy doing with family or friends? Do you still do any of these things?

Strengths-Based Care Management for Older Adults. © 2000, Health Professions Press, Inc.

Essential Components of a Strengths Inventory

Given system barriers such as large caseloads, the strengths assessment process should, at minimum, cover the following items:

- Learn how the client has coped with difficulties in the past.

- Ask the client what he or she wants and needs in life.

- Focus on existing or potential personal and environmental strengths, interests, and resources rather than problems or weaknesses.

Basic questions to ask:

- Who is important to you in your life?

- What do you do to fill your days?

- What makes life worth living for you?

- What is going well for you right now?

Strengths-Based Care Management for Older Adults. © 2000, Health Professions Press, Inc.

Module 4

Care Planning and Implementation

Traditionally, during care planning the care manager identifies the appropriate resources, decides who should provide each service, and arranges the type and frequency of the services to be provided. As time goes on, the care manager evaluates the individual's situation and determines whether any adjustments are needed. However, the traditional approach does not take into consideration the following factors:

- The individual's preferences and stated interests
- The individual's and the caregiver's participation in developing the care plan
- The individual's need for personal planning and goal setting
- The individual's ability to incorporate his or her strengths into the planning process

In traditional care planning the client is the person who is most often neglected in the process or is consulted only perfunctorily to determine his or her satisfaction with services. If the care plan is to be successful, it should reflect the client's goals, wants, and needs. Such cooperation between the older person and his or her care manager will decrease the number of crises and increase the likelihood of successful goal completion.

Research supports the notion that most successful care plans are those in which the client's motivations are directed toward what the care manager is trying to provide. Research conducted at the University of Chicago demonstrated that target problems that were identified by the client or as a result of a close client–care manager agreement showed the most successful results. Goals are well formed when they belong to the client and are expressed in the client's language. Care plans with poor outcomes demonstrated limited "motivational congruence" between care managers and clients (Epstein, 1988).

Client-Driven Care Planning and Implementation

Practitioner-driven plans that prescribe the client's services and goals are considered routine at most long-term care service agencies. Many older people, especially older women, were in a dependent or subordinate position for most of their lives, and their preferences were not taken into account or even acknowledged. These individuals may be hesitant and reluctant to explore their dreams, hopes, and desires.

The goal of personal planning in the strengths model is to begin where the individual is physically and emotionally and move with him or her to higher levels of participation. The care manager's aim is to expand the client's confidence in making choices and selecting options. Decisions made by clients are important, no matter how small, and the care manager's task is to provide such individuals with a continuous array of alternatives.

Enhancing client participation produces a strong payoff in terms of better care plan outcomes. Care managers make fewer poor decisions and experience less anxiety about being the "all-knowing" resource expert. With direction from the client and his or her primary caregivers, the care manager is better able to avoid making detrimental service mistakes.

The first task that the care manager performs in creating a care plan is to break broad goals into manageable parts. Breaking goals into manageable parts involves dissecting them into short-term goals or tasks that specify explicit actions (Rapp, 1998). Once these options are generated, the care manager assists the client in choosing the ones that are the most desirable to pursue. Protecting an older person's right to choose among different alternatives is imperative. In addition, client-directed goal setting helps to demystify the care plan and strengthen the client–care manager relationship.

The Personal Goal Plan

The personal goal plan is a client-driven care plan that helps older people attain what they need and want for their lives. The personal goal plan differs from traditional care plans by blending clients' needs with their wants. Personal and service goals are generated from the client's perception of the areas in which he or she feels motivated to work. The long-term goal is derived from the client's list of priorities in the strengths inventory. The strengths inventory process serves as the vehicle that drives and facilitates the decisions that need to be made to develop the care plan. The plan then becomes a map of the goals to be pursued and the tasks to be addressed (Kisthardt, 1992).

By using the personal care plan, the care manager demonstrates a commitment to the client to take the steps needed to achieve the desired long-term goal. The care manager assumes an active role in helping the client break down long-term goals into smaller short-term tasks or goals. "Case managers must explore whether or not the goal is one which they can do with consumers or whether it would be desirable for them to do it for consumers" (Kisthardt & Rapp, 1992, p. 115). In strengths-based care management *do with* is preferable to *do for*.

The care manager also works with the client to assign responsibilities to possible informal and paid helpers. During subsequent visits, the goals and the helpers are reviewed and modified if necessary. The care plan also specifies helpers outside the individual's immediate support circle who will be a part of the plan (e.g., neighbors, church groups, civic clubs, other community resources).

The personal goal planning process is guided by the belief that people grow by building on successful endeavors in the areas of their lives that hold meaning for them. Even small successes can lead to renewed involvement, personal achievement, and an improved quality of life.

Why Goals Succeed or Fail

Learning Unit 14

Purpose:
To help participants learn the importance of goal setting and the reasons why goals succeed or fail

Approximate Time Required:
30 minutes

Supplies:
Flipchart and marker(s)

Instructions:
1. Ask the following questions and write participant responses on a flipchart:
   •"How are care plans developed at your agency?"
   •"Why are well-defined goals essential to effective care plans?" (Supplement participant responses with the following information: Well-defined goals ensure the efficient use of limited time, effectiveness of achieving desired outcomes, an increase in client hopefulness and motivation to work with the care manager, and an increase in care manager satisfaction.)
   •"Why set goals with older adults?" (Supplement participant responses with the following information. Goal setting helps to define the focus of the helping process, to identify what clients expect from their caregivers, and to clarify what each person can do to help the client achieve his or her goals.)
2. Brainstorm with participants about why goals fail. Ask participants, "How many of you have set goals that weren't achieved? Why did they fail?" Possible participant responses include the following:
   •Goal set too high/overwhelming
   •Goal set too low/client became bored
   •Time involved to achieve goal was unrealistic
   •Lacked needed information to achieve goal

•Goal conflicted with other priorities or client is working on too many goals at one time

•Client is afraid to try or is afraid of the result

•No recognition received for each step accomplished along the way

•Lacked the necessary support to achieve goal

•Goal was not enjoyable or no pleasure was attached to it

•Goal depended on resources that are not available

•Client lacked skills to achieve goal

3. Write participants' reasons for goal failure on a flipchart. Encourage the group to come up with an extensive list. The following questions facilitate the discussion of why goals fail.

•"How many of you make New Year's resolutions?"

•"How many of you followed through on your resolutions?"

•"If not, what happened? Why did the goal fail?"

4. Ask participants whether their reasons for goal failure would resonate with their clients. "Are the responses listed on the flipchart similar to or different from your client's reasons for goal failure?" Integrate the following points into the discussion:

•The reasons that goals fail for our clients are the same reasons that goals fail for all people.

•Psychiatric and physical disabilities may exacerbate the reasons why clients' goals fail.

•The reasons that goals fail usually are dictated by the nature of the goal itself rather than by health or mental problems.

•When clients fail to achieve their desired goals, the care manager should explore the reasons why the plan of action was not successfully attained. Understanding and identifying the barriers that clients are facing and why they are not highly motivated to follow the plan is critical to successful goal achievement.

5. Conclude this learning unit by emphasizing the importance of setting client-specific goals. The strengths model planning methods, as discussed in Learning Units 15 and 16, facilitate increased client goal attainment. Indicators of successful goal achievement that are explored further in Units 15 and 16 include the following:

•The client has a sense of ownership of the plan.

•The goals are broken down into clear and concrete behavioral steps.

•The goals are not in conflict with competing priorities and demands.

•A match exists between the goals and the person's skills and available resources.

Developing Goals that Work

Purpose:
To help participants understand and apply standards to goal statements during personal goal planning

Approximate Time Required:
45 minutes

Supplies:
Make photocopies of the handouts "Standards for Successful Goals" and "Sample Participant Goals" (see pp. 65 and 66); pencils or pens

Instructions:
1. Distribute and review each standard on the handout "Standards for Successful Goals."
   Incorporate additional examples if needed before moving into the exercise.
2. Distribute the handout "Sample Participant Goals" and ask participants to apply the
   goal-setting standards to each of the goals. The handout includes poorly written and
   well-written goal statements. If the goal fails to meet the applied standard, then encourage participants to write a short-term goal statement that does meet the criteria.
   (The majority of the goal statements in the "Sample Participant Goals" handout fail
   to meet one or more of the standards.)
3. In a full group discussion, ask individual participants to share their answers. A wide
   range of possible alternatives exist for reshaping the goals to better meet the five characteristics of successful goals. Discuss a number of possible options for each short-
   term goal that fails to meet the established standards (Kisthardt, Gowdy, & Rapp,
   1992). Explain to participants why each goal does or does not meet the standards for
   successful goals, and encourage participants to add to the following reasons for goal
   failure:
   - *"Joe understands why he needs to stop yelling at his homemaker."* This goal is not stated
     in positive terms, nor is the goal behaviorally focused. "Joe says a kind word to his
     homemaker each week" would meet these two standards.
   - *"The care manager will provide ongoing support to Anna."* This goal is not understand-
     able and meaningful to the client, nor is it specific. Does Anna know what support
     is or in what form it will be given to her? A better example is "The care manager will
     call once a week to talk with Anna about how she is feeling."

- *"Wilma will walk three times a week with a friend."* The way in which this goal is stated is not wrong, but it could be more specific by including the name of the friend with whom Wilma will walk on a weekly basis.
- *"Sam will wear his medical alert when he goes to the bathroom."* This goal is specific, positive, behavioral, and understandable to the client. The question in this goal lies in the probability of success for goal achievement. Sam probably will not remember to wear the medical alert every time he goes to the bathroom. However, if Sam has fallen multiple times in the bathroom and refuses to wear his medical alert in his home, then stating the goal in terms of the bathroom is a good place to begin for this client.
- *"Sarah will prepare a hot meal when her homemaker is present."* This goal is positive, measurable, specific, and understandable. The goal could be improved by including a time frame, especially if Sarah loves to cook but has repeatedly left on the gas stove-top burner and the bottoms of her pans have burned.
- *"Doris will stop smoking when she is on oxygen."* Goals do not have a high probability of success for an individual with an addiction. In addition, the goal statement is not written in specific or positive terms. A goal statement that is observable, specific, and has a high probability of success is "Doris will smoke each day without wearing her oxygen mask after she eats supper with her sister."
- *"Frances is going to work on her socialization needs."* This goal fails because it is not understandable, specific, or observable. Frances most likely does not know what is meant by "socialization needs" or what she should be doing to meet this goal. An example of a goal with a higher likelihood of success is "Frances will attend a weekly book club hosted by her friend, Sally."

Using the Personal Goal Plan

Learning Unit 16

Purpose:
To help participants master the knowledge and skills needed to develop goals and conduct a personal goal plan

Approximate Time Required:
60 minutes

Supplies:

"Ann's Strengths Inventory" (overhead transparency from Module 3); make an overhead transparency of "Ann's Personal Goal Plan"; make photocopies and an overhead transparency of the handout "Personal Goal Plan (Sample)"; make photocopies of the handouts "Guidelines for Conducting a Personal Goal Plan" and "Overseeing the Personal Goal Plan" (see pp. 67–70); flipchart and marker

Instructions:

1. Ask participants to use the Module 3 handout "Ann's Strengths Inventory" (or display the overhead transparency that you made for Module 3) to identify one of Ann's wants as reflected in her list of priorities.

2. Write in the space for long-term goals the priority that is identified by the group on the personal goal plan overhead. Ask the group under what domain or domains this priority would fall and to check the box on the personal goal plan.

3. Ask participants to brainstorm a list of possible options for meeting Ann's long-term goal by using the strengths and resources listed on the overhead. For example, the group could choose Ann's long-term goal "I want to have some fun." Encourage group members to generate an expansive list of options and write them on the flipchart. The following are ways to help Ann to meet her goal:
    •Teach a college art class.
    •Volunteer with an afterschool elementary art program.
    •Join and participate in senior aerobics.
    •Help organize an art fair.
    •Join and participate in an art association.

4. Ask the group to identify possible naturally occurring resources, friends, and social supports that can help Ann to achieve her long-term goal priorities.

5. Display the overhead transparency "Ann's Personal Goal Plan." Discuss how Ann's plan demonstrates the ways to break down a long-term goal into small, concrete, specific action steps. Emphasize to the group that the action steps are accomplished by Ann or by Ann along with her care manager.

6. Present the four components of defining action steps:
    •Which activities occur in *what* order?
    •*Who* is responsible?
    •*When* does each activity take place?
    •*Where* does each activity occur?
    Action steps should be stated in positive terms with target dates set within 1 week for review or completion. As short-term goal statements are written, care managers

must ensure that they meet the standards discussed in Learning Unit 15 ("Standards for Successful Goals").

7. Discuss possible quotes from Ann or Ann's care manager that were used in the Comments column of Ann's personal goal plan to demonstrate how the plan is an ongoing process.

8. Summarize the following guidelines for conducting a personal goal plan as participants look over the handouts "Personal Goal Plan (Sample)" and "Guidelines for Conducting a Personal Goal Plan":

   • The long-term goal should reflect something the person wants, needs, and hopes for as reflected in the "Individual's Desires/Aspirations" column on the strengths inventory.

   • The short-term goals or action steps are broken down into specific, concrete steps and reflect the client's own language.

   • The steps are written in positive, behavioral terms and indicate what the client will do, not what he or she will stop doing.

   • The strengths and resources listed on the strengths inventory are integrated into the goals and tasks of the personal goal plan.

   • The client is assigned more responsibility than the care manager or other helpers in the support system.

   • Time frames are established with each step. Short-term goals should cover periods of not longer than 3–6 months and should be reviewed on a weekly or biweekly basis.

   • The personal goal plan is continually revised and updated as the goals are reviewed.

   • Continuous praise and encouragement are given to reinforce ongoing client participation. Rewards and celebrations occur when goals are accomplished.

9. Distribute the handout "Overseeing the Personal Goal Plan," and review and discuss it with participants. Highlight the importance of updating the personal goal plan at each contact with clients. Each contact should include celebrating accomplishments, identifying barriers, and suggesting new tasks and resources to ensure that short-term goals are accomplished.

10. Conclude the exercise by pointing out that participants are free to adapt and modify the strengths inventory and the personal goal plan to meet their individual agency's needs. Encourage participants to integrate these tools into their agency's forms or to use the tools as a supplement to or instead of existing assessment and planning forms. The strengths inventory and personal goal plan are to be perceived as tools that care managers can use to help their clients achieve their goals, not as burdens to add to their existing paperwork.

Standards for Successful Goals

1. **Stated in positive terms**

   Stated in terms of what clients are <u>going to do</u> rather than what they are <u>going to stop doing</u>.

   For example: *Susan will call her daughter when she is low on groceries.*

2. **High probability of success**

   Each goal must be realistic and achievable. Artificial ceilings should not be placed on clients to prevent goal failure. Client investment and commitment is critical to goal achievement.

   For example: *Fran will use her walker when she retrieves her dog from outside.*

3. **Measurable and observable**

   Goals should have a visible and explicit outcome. Each goal should reflect only one behavioral step.

   For example: *Fred will take his medications each night during the evening news.*

4. **Specific, small, and time limited**

   Short-term goals should be time limited—no longer than 3 months—and broken down into small steps. A reasonable time frame increases the probability that goals will be achieved.

   For example: *Jenny will attend senior aerobics twice a week at the senior center.*

5. **Understandable and meaningful to the client**

   Clients' ownership of the personal planning process increases when goals are relevant to their needs and reflect as much as possible their own language.

   For example: *Rita will call Mrs. Smith each week for a ride to her sewing circle.*

Strengths-Based Care Management for Older Adults. © 2000 Health Professions Press, Inc.

Sample Participant Goals

1. Joe understands why he needs to stop yelling at his homemaker.

2. The care manager will provide ongoing support to Anna.

3. Wilma will walk three times a week with a friend.

4. Sam will wear his medical alert when he goes to the bathroom.

5. Sarah will prepare a hot meal when her homemaker is present.

6. Doris will stop smoking when she is on oxygen.

7. Frances is going to work on her socialization needs.

Personal Goal Plan (Sample)

For: _____ Case Manager: _____ Date: _____

Planned Frequency of Contact: _____

Life Domain Focused On:

❏ Daily Living Situation	❏ Social Supports
❏ Health	❏ Spirituality/Religion
❏ Finances/Insurance	❏ Leisure/Recreational Interests

My Long-Term Goal:

Short-Term Goals (Tasks)	Who's Responsible	Target Date	Date Accomplished	Comments

_____ _____
Client's signature   Date

_____ _____
Care manager's signature   Date

_____ _____
Collateral signature   Date

Strengths-Based Care Management for Older Adults. © 2000 Health Professions Press, Inc.

Ann's Personal Goal Plan

For: __**Ann**__   Case Manager: __**Sally P.**__   Date: __**7/16/2000**__

Planned Frequency of Contact: __**1x week**__

Life Domain Focused On:

[X] Daily Living Situation	[ ] Social Supports
[ ] Health	[ ] Spirituality/Religion
[ ] Finances/Insurance	[ ] Leisure/Recreational Interests

My Long-Term Goal:
"I would like to move to a larger apartment."

Short-Term Goals (Tasks)	Who's Responsible	Target Date	Date Accomplished	Comments
1) **Call HUD office to request Section 8 application.**	**Ann**	**6/24/00**	**6/23/00**	**Ann has the paperwork.**
2) **Fill out application for Section 8.**	**Ann & Sally**	**7/3/00**	**7/1/00**	**"Wow, I'm glad Sally helped me."**
3) **Turn in Section 8 application, and meet with local housing authority.**	**Ann & Sally**	**7/5/00**	**7/2/00**	**"Good job, Ann, on telling the manager what you needed!"**
4) **Call prospective landlords to set up appointments to look at apts.**	**Ann**	**7/14/00**	**7/10/00**	**"Way to go, Ann, on finding a list of pet-friendly apartments!"**
5) **Ask landlords if they accept pets.**	**Ann**	**7/14/00**	**7/14/00**	
6) **Call Rita (sister) for transportation to look at apts.**	**Ann**	**7/16/00**	**7/16/00**	

_____		_____	
Client's signature	Date	Care manager's signature	Date
		_____	
		Collateral signature	Date

Strengths-Based Care Management for Older Adults. © 2000 Health Professions Press, Inc.

Guidelines for Conducting a Personal Goal Plan

- The long-term goal should reflect something the person wants, needs, and hopes for as reflected in the "Individual's Desires/Aspirations" column on the strengths inventory.
- The short-term goals or action steps are broken down into specific, concrete steps and reflect the client's own language.
- The steps are written in positive, behavioral terms and indicate what the client will do, not what he or she will stop doing.
- The strengths and resources listed on the strengths inventory are integrated into the goals and tasks of the personal goal plan.
- The client is assigned more responsibility than the care manager or other helpers in the support system.
- Time frames are established with each step. Short-term goals should cover periods of not longer than 3–6 months and should be reviewed on a weekly or biweekly basis.
- The personal plan is continually revised and updated as the goals are reviewed.
- Continuous praise and encouragement are given to reinforce ongoing client participation. Rewards and celebrations occur when goals are accomplished.

Ask yourself the following questions:

Does the long-term goal clearly reflect what is asked for on the strengths inventory?

Are your action steps broken down into small steps?

Are the short-term steps written in positive language?

Can you describe exactly who is doing what?

Are resources, strengths, and information from your strengths inventory reflected in the goal plan?

Are dates specified when action steps will be completed?

Is goal progress reflected in the Comments section?

Is your personal goal plan signed and dated?

Overseeing the Personal Goal Plan

Follow-up care management visits should include a discussion of

What has been accomplished since the last session
Which tasks need to be continued
Which tasks can be abandoned
Which tasks need to be changed

Remember to encourage and praise the client for tasks accomplished.

If a task was not carried out, ask what happened.

Was the person not sufficiently prepared to implement the task?
Was the task beyond the client's abilities?
Was there a misunderstanding?

If the task didn't meet the client's need, explore these questions:

What part went wrong?
What could have been done differently?

When a task has been successfully completed, review what worked and encourage the client to use a similar process in the future.

Strengths-Based Care Management for Older Adults. © 2000, Health Professions Press, Inc.

Resource Acquisition

Securing and Sustaining Resources

The strengths perspective is an alternative conception of the environment in which "typical" and "naturally occurring" resources (e.g., family, friends, youth groups, civic clubs) are pursued assertively before paid services are used. The environment is viewed as an abundant source of opportunities, resources, and people (Sullivan, 1989). Therefore, the primary task of the strengths model care manager is to break down the sometimes-overwhelming series of obstacles that separate clients from their community's resources.

Strengths model care managers believe naturally occurring resources are present in the community and are devoted to making them more accessible, accommodating, available, and adequate for clients. Naturally occurring helpers include a collective of supporters with whom the client comes in contact regularly, such as neighbors, grocery store clerks, and friends. Amidst identifying and accessing naturally occurring helpers, the care manager acknowledges that immediate family members often are exhausted from the profound impact of sustaining the older person within the community (Tice & Perkins, 1996).

The strengths model posits that behavior is a function of the resources that are available to an individual. In this view all people have a right to use the resources of society. The challenge for the care manager lies in deciding how to assist a client or group in obtaining its rights and resources.

Advocacy

Influencing resource people and networks on behalf of clients is an essential component of strengths-based practice. To establish, ensure, and receive the needed benefits or services, it is imperative for care managers to effectively influence key actors, such as landlords, doctors, and insurance agents, who control resources.

Operationalizing an advocacy perspective requires care managers to have extensive knowledge of community resources and supportive social services that are desired by older people. Care managers also must have the technical expertise to link the resources quickly and in a manner that is consistent with the preferences of their clients and their clients' primary caregivers.

Advocacy can be understood as any specific behavior in which one engages to influence stakeholders in the community to make a desired resource available. The care manager and the client must determine what the desired available resources are and then identify the specific organization or person in control of the particular resource. Advocacy efforts are used to influence social services and medical, legal, and mental health systems to be more responsive to clients' resource preferences (Sullivan & Fisher, 1994).

Experienced care managers know that helping clients reach and maintain their goals can be the most difficult part of care management. Successful advocacy efforts help clients and their support system gain needed resources such as affordable housing and in-home care services or help them to become involved in social activities. Influencing the people in control of the resources on behalf of clients behooves care managers to ask themselves questions based on the four dimensions of advocacy: is the resource *available, accessible,* and *adequate*? and is there *accommodation* (Rapp, 1998)?

The first step in the advocacy process is to identify the availability of a given resource. For example, are service or business groups available to assist with yard work and home repair needs?

The second step in the advocacy process is to identify any obstacles to accessibility, such as lack of transportation or steep stairways. These obstacles may prevent a resource option from being available to the client.

The third step in the advocacy process is to identify how adequately an acquired resource meets the needs of a particular client. For example, does the client's housing situation meet minimal standards for safety such as heating, cooling, and protection from pest infestation?

The final step is that care managers must consider how accommodating the resource will be. For example, an older client with difficulty hearing becomes extremely frustrated when the taxicab driver he calls to take him to the grocery store leaves after honking the horn once. This resource was not at all accommodating. Consequently, addressing accommodation issues frequently involves educating the people who control the resources.

The strengths model conception of resource acquisition and advocacy requires care managers to represent the interests of older adults as if they were their own. The interests are the needs and wants that are identified through the strengths inventory and the personal goal planning process. Advocacy strategies are crafted together after the care manager has a clear understanding of the client's prioritized needs and preferences. Tangible action to change the status of the resource is built on the strengths of the older person (Rapp, 1998).

Undoubtedly, there will never be enough paid services to meet clients' needs. However, focusing on the problems, deficits, and lacks in the social environment without moving assertively to increase resources can further restrict the number of helping resources. Simply having a belief in the potential of the environment and assertively pursuing options other than formal services increases the sheer number of the available helping resources (Sullivan, 1992).

Mapping Your Support System

Purpose:

To increase participants' knowledge about how to recruit naturally occurring helpers to help clients achieve their goals

Approximate Time Required:

30 minutes

Supplies:

Blank paper, pencils or pens; flipchart and marker

Instructions:

1. Demonstrate on a flipchart how to draw one large circle with three more circles inside one another, each subsequent circle getting smaller (the drawing will look like a target).

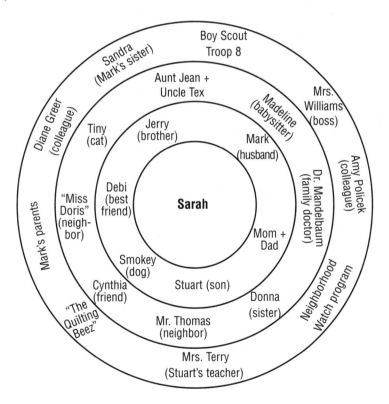

2. Distribute blank paper to all participants, and ask them to draw the four circles on it.

3. Ask participants to write their name in the middle of the smallest circle, which is in the middle of the drawing.

4. After circulating around the room to make sure everyone has drawn his or her four circles correctly, explain the importance of the circles encircling the person's name: Each circle represents a level of closeness or intimacy within a person's support system. Eventually, the circles will be filled with the names of people, groups, professionals, organizations, and even animals that are important to the participant's life at this moment.

5. Ask participants to write down the names of the individuals or groups that they feel so close to that it is hard to imagine life without them. The names should be placed in the inner circle (the one next to the participant's name).

6. Ask the participants to write in the next circle (the one within the outermost circle) the names of the people or social supports that are still important to them but that they do not feel quite as close to as the names in the previous circle.

7. Ask participants to write in the outer circle the names of people or groups with whom they are in contact on a regular basis but are not in a close, intimate relationship. The names listed in this circle should be social supports, whether friends, relatives, civic clubs, doctors, or professional colleagues who have not been mentioned in the other circles. Allow participants about 5–10 minutes to complete the assignment.

8. Ask participants to share whom they listed in their personal support network and where they placed these individuals in their support network.

9. Lead a discussion on how different and similar the participant support networks were within the group and among the group and their clients. The points listed here should be integrated within the discussion:
   • "What did you learn about your support system?"
   • "Where did you place traditional informal supports such as family members, relatives, and friends in the intimacy continuum?"
   • "Where did you place other professionals in your network?"
   • "Where do you think your clients place professional helpers?"
   • "Did you find any surprises?"
   • "What are the strengths or weaknesses of your system?"
   • "How is your support system similar to or different from your clients' systems?"

10. Conclude the exercise by encouraging participants to use this exercise with their clients to help them better understand their client's social support system and the meaning and value that are attached to these supports. This mapping exercise can be useful to introduce discussions of living wills by asking one's client, "If you lost your ability to talk, who would you want to provide your care?"

Discussion Points:

- As compared with younger adults, older adults have lost a significant number of their inner circle relationships because of death, children growing up and moving away, friends transitioning to retirement housing, and so forth. The relationships and the support systems on which they have relied for most of their life are no longer immediately available to provide support. Subsequently, they draw on outer circle or less intimate relationships to provide help.
- Professional helpers move to the inner circle level of importance as older people's traditional caregivers (e.g., adult children) are no longer available to provide support.
- Caregivers listed in the inner circles may move their relationship with an older person to a lower level of closeness or to the outer circle by distancing, either physically or emotionally. Caregiver burnout or exhaustion often can be observed as older people's emotional and physical needs become more demanding.
- Homebound older adults are not able to develop new social relationships or even maintain former relationships as do younger adults or active older people. Active older people are able to build a variety of connections to draw on for support through volunteer work, part-time employment, hobbies, and/or interaction with their family's activities. Developing social support options outside those of professional helpers becomes increasingly limited as health and functional status diminish.
- Inner circle relationships, such as immediate family members and relatives, typically are thought of as the first line of physical or emotional support. Care managers should not assume that their older clients would automatically draw on those relationships for custodial or emotional support. Older people may more readily choose less intimate relationships to provide support services because of a long-standing family conflict, a deep sense of pride, or experience of some form of abuse in their close relationships.

Naturally Occurring Helpers

Learning Unit 18

Purpose:
To increase participants' skills in identifying a range of naturally occurring helpers and in-service monitoring

Approximate Time Required:
45 minutes

Supplies:

Make photocopies and an overhead transparency of the handout "The Strengths Approach to Resource Acquisition" (see p. 84); overhead projector and blank transparencies; flipchart and marker

Instructions:

1. Display the transparency "The Strengths Approach to Resource Acquisition" on the overhead projector. Review with participants the core components of strengths-based resource acquisition. Resource acquisition from a strengths approach requires
   •Considering naturally occurring helpers and resources before formal services
   •Viewing the community as an oasis of potential resources
   •Using assertive outreach to total community resources as the preferred model of intervention
2. Solicit a list of naturally occurring community resources from the group. Write the list on a blank overhead or on the flipchart.
3. Discuss the possible advantages and disadvantages of incorporating naturally occurring community resources into a client's care plan.

   ### Advantages:

   They often are more accessible because eligibility requirements are less burdensome or strict.
   Naturally occurring helpers lack stigma.
   Naturally occurring resources usually are cheaper or more cost-effective.
   Trust is more readily established when the services are provided by a known caregiver.

   ### Disadvantages:

   Collecting and gaining access to naturally occurring resources are more time consuming for the care manager than for him or her to rely on formally constituted services.
   Using informal networks requires ongoing contact with and outreach to a diverse range of community resources.
   Finding naturally occurring resources can be difficult and complex.
   Identifying and using naturally occurring helpers require a high level of expertise and skill in developing and nurturing informal helping relationships.
4. Continue the discussion by presenting reasons why naturally occurring helpers are more favorable and acceptable to many older clients than are formal services. The reasons why older adults often resist formal services include

•Maintains clients' illusion of independence: For example, an older woman tells her neighbor, "My daughter came for lunch today," but she omits any reference to the fact that her daughter may have brought groceries, put them away, made lunch, washed and dried clothes, and cleaned the bathroom while she was there. Help from family members usually is viewed as a favor, whereas services performed by a stranger are a vivid reminder of dependence. Giving older people choices, such as whom to hire and what he or she will be doing, helps them maintain some control over their lives.

•Fears about depleting finances: Many older people worry about running out of money, even if that fear is unjustified. Using funds to pay for in-home services is an acknowledgment of financial vulnerability and the fact that the final stages of life are upon them. One way to diffuse their fear is to add up the amount of money that would be spent for a defined number of hours weekly for 1 year and compare that with their total assets; this should show them that ample funds remain for the future. Families also can reassure their older loved one that having their present needs taken care of is far more important to them than their inheritance for future luxuries.

•Lack of supervisory skills: Most older people have never used paid helpers in their homes and simply do not know how to supervise them. Helping them to devise a written list of everything they would like to have done and to routinely communicate with and give the homemaker guidance will help ease their minds. Encouraging older people to praise their homemaker for work done well also is important.

•Fear of victimization: Having a stranger in their home while they are alone can be frightening to older people. People with poor eyesight, hearing, or memory can feel particularly vulnerable. Family members can offer to be present in the house while the paid helper is there to give the older person time to build trust with the helper. This also gives families enough time to become acquainted with the array of in-home paid helpers and to form their own impressions of the helper's competence and reliability.

•Reduced contact with family: Older adults may fear that in-home help will influence family members to come over or see them less often. Family members should listen to those fears and reassure their older loved one that their need for respite from caregiving tasks will not take away from their relationship.

5. After facilitating a discussion of the advantages of using naturally occurring helpers, talk about the importance of monitoring and sustaining these services. Include the following points:

- Monitoring is the process of evaluating the progress that has been made toward some clearly established outcome. It also is simply checking in with one's clients on a regular basis to see how they are doing.
- Typically, monitoring is accomplished with progress notes or quarterly reviews. This practice does not, however, capture the range of activities that are necessary to help clients sustain the gains that they have made during their involvement with a care manager.
- Monitoring is a function shared with the client in the strengths perspective. The goal is to empower clients to monitor themselves, to use others in their social networks to get the feedback they need and want, and to help them recognize the control that they can exert over their own lives.

6. Illustrate monitoring as defined in the strengths model—the "3 Cs" (Collective, Continuing, Collaboration) review of the helping process. Draw a triangle on a flipchart or blank overhead transparency, and write the words "collective," "continuing," and "collaboration" on each axis of the triangle.

7. After illustrating the 3 Cs, point to the first side of the triangle and define the word "collective."

Collective: To help clients sustain the gains that they have made, a collective of supports and supporters needs to be developed.

8. Ask participants what strategies they have used to identify the nonpaid helpers in their clients' lives.

9. Present the following points regarding the importance of paid helpers in a client's collective of supports:
- Many older people do not recognize special assistance when it comes from someone in an employment situation because help is extended subtly.
- The client's family may discover that the client has more social contact than they thought possible, or they may discover that their loved one exhibits a totally different personality outside the home.

10. Elicit examples of helpers in employment roles from participants and methods for identifying them. (*Suggestions:* Encourage family members to introduce themselves to local business owners; accompany their relative through a typical day to learn what help is given, by whom, and how often; or accompany their relative to a restaurant or to the hairdresser.) Examples of employment helpers include health care professionals (e.g., nurses, doctors, home health aides), bus drivers, apartment managers, grocery store clerks, postal carriers, taxicab drivers, pharmacists, hairdressers and barbers, and restaurant staff.

11. Ask participants how they give recognition to their clients' naturally occurring helpers. For example, families can acknowledge helpers in employment roles by giving gifts, sending letters of appreciation to their supervisors, inviting them to speak up when the older person's needs begin to exceed the helper's time constraints, supporting them verbally, or letting them know what others in the informal network are doing.

12. Point to the second side of the triangle and define the word "continuing."

Continuing:
- Even after the client has achieved a goal, a lot of work needs to be done to sustain that goal. Therefore, continuing contact is maintained not only with the client but also with family and other key people in the collective of caring to meet the wants and needs of everyone in the collective.
- The goal of contacting naturally occurring helpers on a continuing basis is to strengthen their ability to provide assistance to the members of their networks as well as to reach out to other individuals. This linkage encourages establishing partnerships to help identify community strengths, unmet needs, and obstacles to effective service delivery.
- The care manager's job is to provide direction, resolve conflicts, model certain behaviors, and teach skills to clients and caregivers. For example, a neighbor agrees to provide a daily respite break for the primary caregiver. To maintain and sustain this helping relationship, the respite volunteer needs regular and frequent communication with the care manager. The volunteer also may need ongoing help, information, and support, including recognition of his or her efforts.

13. Point to the third side of the triangle and define the word "collaboration."

Collaboration:
- Collaboration is forming partnerships to recognize the value of each person's input and the benefits of making the helping experience advantageous for everyone.
- Although care management is thought to be the most effective tool because it offers person-to-person contact, the care manager's time is limited. Therefore, care managers must learn to recruit community collaborators. Some community collaborators who often are overlooked include businesspeople, educators, clergy, recreation directors, service clubs, retired older adults, and older clients themselves. Examples of resource development that results from successful collaboration with these naturally occurring helpers are provided in upcoming learning units.
- Neither naturally occurring helpers nor paid professionals have all of the expertise and resources that are needed to solve problems and meet needs. By forming part-

nerships and becoming collaborators with these community helpers, new and innovative approaches to service delivery can be developed.

•One of the most important functions served by nonpaid community collaborators is the link to community resources. Establishing an advisory board or resource council is an excellent way to identify and develop relationships with a diverse range of naturally occurring helpers.

Advocacy in Action

Purpose:
To help participants understand what advocacy is and how they can be better advocates for their clients

Approximate Time Required:
30 minutes

Supplies:
Make photocopies and an overhead transparency of the handout "The Four 'As' of Advocacy"; make photocopies of the handouts "Advocating for Success" and "Sample Responses for 'Advocating for Success'" (make fewer copies of the latter handout and offer copies to any participant who is particularly interested in it or wants to use it as a prompt); make photocopies of the "Advocacy in Action Worksheets" (see pp. 85–89)

Instructions:
1. Distribute the handout "The Four 'As' of Advocacy" and discuss it using the overhead transparency. Explain to participants that as with the "3 'Cs'" of the helping process, advocacy has four components. Present the following information:
    •**Availability:** What resources are available in the community, in the client's neighborhood, and so forth that could help the client to meet his or her needs? Generate as many possibilities with the client as possible. Consider who controls the resources, whether these individual agencies have direct control over the resources or are part of a larger decision-making process, and to whom the resources will respond best: the client, you, or an agency administrator.
    •**Accessibility:** Obstacles, such as lack of transportation or steep stairways, may prevent a resource from being useful for the client. After identifying the obstacles, de-

cide how and with whom the care manager or the client could advocate for the removal of these obstacles.

• **Accommodation:** Once the areas of availability and accessibility have been satisfied, the care manager must consider how accommodating the resource will be. Accommodation entails the kind of interaction and communication the client will have with the resource. For example, an older client may have a hard time walking through the grocery store to shop. Many stores provide motorized shopping carts for people with disabilities. If the client's local grocery does not have these carts, then perhaps the store's manager would be willing to purchase them if the care manager and the client approached him or her. Addressing accommodation issues frequently involves educating the person or people in control of the resource. (Emphasize to participants that they must be very careful not to sever relationships or partnerships [collaboration] with resource providers. Care managers and clients should advocate in nonthreatening ways, not only for the sake of their present clients but also for all future clients who may use that resource.)

• **Adequacy:** Does the resource meet the needs of the client and help him or her meet a goal? For example, does an older person's lawn and garden service meet his or her personal standards and those of the neighborhood for yard care? If not, how will the care manager and/or the client advocate with the contractors to get what the client needs? (Emphasize to participants that when care managers contact a resource, they should keep their clients informed as to progress so that clients feel part of the process. When a client contacts a resource, he or she should give the resource positive feedback for all efforts, whether they are successful or not.)

2. Form small groups of three to four people. Distribute the handout "Advocating for Success" to the groups. Ask the groups to identify the specific advocacy actions and behaviors that have achieved successful outcomes for their clients, and identify which of the four "As" of advocacy have been implemented. (For example, after the client and care manager from Module 4 contacted the taxicab company about the client's inability to hear the cab's horn, drivers were instructed to get out of their cabs, go to clients' front doors, and knock or ring doorbells when clients requested such service.) Note successes as well as failures. Group answers can be recorded on the handout. Allow 20 minutes for this exercise.

3. Reconvene the full group and share responses. The handout "Sample Responses for 'Advocating for Success'" can be shared with the large group or you can use it as your presenter's points.

4. Collect the lists developed by the group. Photocopy the lists during a break, and at the end of the training, hand back a copy of each list to the participants.

5. Ask the large group to get back into their small groups. Distribute one of the two "Advocacy in Action Worksheet" care scenarios to each small group. These worksheets can be used as a supplement to or as a replacement for "The Four 'As' of Advocacy" activity. Ask the groups to read their case study and record their responses to each question. Allow 15–20 minutes for this activity.

6. Ask each group to read its answers to the full group. As the small groups share their answers, you may need to push the groups to focus on solutions rather than on barriers when confronting systemic problems. If participants complain that the case study fails to give them enough information, then encourage participants to discern possible clues from their experiences in working with similar situations.

7. Conclude the exercise by reinforcing the group's ability to identify solutions to the environmental obstacles presented in the case studies. In addition, point out the group's creativity in helping the clients acquire the needed services and resources.

Resource Development

Purpose:
To provide participants with the knowledge and skills needed to initiate and develop community resources

Approximate Time Required:
45 minutes

Supplies:
Make photocopies of the handouts "Identifying and Mobilizing Community Resources" and "Successful Community Resource Development Ideas" (see pp. 90–92) and make an overhead transparency of the "Identifying" handout; overhead projector and marker or flipchart and marker; pencils or pens

Instructions:
1. Divide the group into geographical (e.g., urban, rural) or agency groups, and assign a recorder for each group. Give each group a copy of the handout "Identifying and Mobilizing Community Resources," and ask the participants to devise a plan to develop a needed resource for their area. Display the handout questions on an overhead transparency or a flipchart. Allow approximately 30 minutes for brainstorming.

**Learning
Unit 20**

2. Ask the recorder from each small group to report to the larger group and facilitate a discussion of his or her group's ideas. The handout "Successful Community Development Ideas" should be used after the brainstorming session to provide participants with additional resource-development ideas.

3. Conclude the activity by highlighting how the participants operationalized the strengths model resource acquisition through their suggested ideas. Write on a blank overhead transparency or on the flipchart the identified strategies that influenced community providers and expanded clients' access to naturally occurring resources.

The Strengths Approach to Resource Acquisition

Considering naturally occurring helpers and resources before formal services

Viewing the community as an oasis of potential resources

Using assertive outreach to total community resources as the preferred model of intervention

The Four "As" of Advocacy

Availability—What resources are available to help meet your client's unmet needs?

Accessibility—What obstacles might make this resource unusable?

Accommodation—How does your client interact with this resource?

Adequacy—Does this resource meet your client's needs adequately?

Advocating for Success

1. How have you found and obtained resources for your clients?

2. How have you encouraged clients to advocate for themselves?

3. How have you advocated with people in your agency and/or with local, state, or federal agencies about your programs, clients, or both?

Sample Responses for "Advocating for Success"

1. How have you found and obtained resources for your clients?
   - Installed a ramp for a disabled person with donated lumber and donated labor from retired carpenters
   - Created prescription drug program that allowed clients to access the various indigent patient programs
   - Developed a resource list for community medical providers to hand out to patients
   - Advocated on behalf of the client for housing repairs
   - Borrowed money from a local church to purchase new pipes for client's home until she was granted a FHA loan
   - Advocated at a traffic safety program for better-quality transportation system
   - Negotiated with physician to use an alternate home health agency when client was labeled "difficult" and rejected for services

2. How have you encouraged clients to advocate for themselves?
   - Encouraged clients to speak to whomever they are having trouble with
   - Assisted clients with contacting their legislators so that they could advocate for themselves
   - Suggested that clients speak up to their physicians concerning their health problems/needs
   - Assisted clients with locating resources and supported them while they made contacts
   - Assisted clients with purchasing Yellow Cab discount booklets
   - Educated clients about existing resources available to them
   - Assisted client with prioritizing medical bills and establishing a payment schedule
   - Encouraged and supported clients' appeals for SSI/Medicaid

3. How have you advocated with people in your agency and/or with local, state, or federal agencies about your programs, clients, or both?
   - Bartered with various organizations (example: for wheelchair repair when Medicaid did not pay the entire cost)
   - Negotiated with utility company to reduce the water bill of a client who encountered repair problems
   - Advocated consistently with utility company until repairs were made for leaks and a budget plan established

Advocacy in Action Worksheet

Bill and Susan Anders are in their 80s. Susan, who has a history of poor health, was hospitalized with severe pain, some mental confusion, and weight loss. She was found to have cancer. After several weeks of hospitalization, she was ready to be discharged. Her physician recommended nursing facility placement.

Susan wears a urinary catheter and requires assistance with eating, dressing, and bathing. At times, she is not mentally alert. During their 60 years of marriage, Bill never provided custodial care or took care of any household chores—he felt that was Susan's domain. Recently, Susan initiated homemaker services from an Area Agency on Aging care manager to help her with heavy cleaning tasks. The hospital staff feels that Bill would not be able to care for his wife on her return home.

Bill absolutely refuses nursing facility placement. He and his wife have been together for almost 60 years, and he refuses to desert her now. He insists on taking her home, where he will care for her in their two-bedroom home. He feels this is what his wife would want and he will not consider any other options. He seems fully alert and is able to comprehend the choices that exist. The physicians and floor staff feel that Bill should not even lift his wife. Bill's care manager from the Area Agency on Aging has been asked to see Bill to try to talk some sense into him. The hospital nurse decided, in consultation with the physician, without Bill's approval, and without consulting Sandy Thompson, their care manager, to initiate a short-term placement for Susan at a local nursing facility.

What is the problem within the system?

What are some possible solutions to this problem?

What agency and/or individual has the power to solve this problem?

What is the chain of command in the agency that has power over this problem?

What should be Sandy's first step in advocating for Bill and Susan's desires and rights?

Strengths-Based Care Management for Older Adults. © 2000 Health Professions Press, Inc.

Advocacy in Action Worksheet

Mrs. Ruby Jones lives alone in a small rundown, cluttered home. She is 79 years old and was widowed within the last 2 years. She is very independent, persistent, and determined to remain in her home, saying, "I would prefer to die in my own bed, thank you."

Ruby has gained a reputation as "difficult" with numerous home health agencies that have worked with her. She dislikes the way the homemakers continually complain about her messy house, and she gets quite angry if anyone suggests that she needs to clean up the newspapers, boxes, and "dumpster treasures" that create narrow pathways through most of her home. Her current home health agency refuses to serve her because of her packrat tendencies. The agency has told her that she is a health and safety risk to their staff and that they have no obligation to serve her.

Ruby's care manager, Sandy Thompson, from the Area Agency on Aging, is very frustrated with trying to maintain Ruby's services—nurses, Meals-On-Wheels, personal care aides, and homemakers. At this point, Sandy is afraid that she will not be able to find another home health agency to serve Ruby. Fortunately, the agency's friendly visitor, a young college student named Michelle, gets along very well with Ruby. Ruby frequently comments on how much she looks forward to Michelle's weekly visits. She often says that she enjoys clearing off a space at the dinner table for Michelle.

What is the problem within the system?

What are some possible solutions to this problem?

What agency and/or individual has the power to solve this problem?

What is the chain of command in the agency that has power over this problem?

What should be Sandy's first step in advocating for Ruby in this situation?

Strengths-Based Care Management for Older Adults. © 2000 Health Professions Press, Inc.

Identifying and Mobilizing Community Resources

The following questions should stimulate the brainstorming process. Answer the questions that are applicable to the resource that you would like to develop.

◆ What kind of resource do you want to develop? (Examples: Car pools, police-operated emergency notification system) What will this resource look like?

◆ How will the resource benefit clients (who will be doing what)?

◆ Who/what organization controls this resource in the community?

◆ Does this person or agency have the authority to make a decision?

◆ Does this person or agency have allies in the community who are influential?

◆ What obstacles could hinder the development of this resource? How will you advocate for the removal of these obstacles?

◆ What is the best way to influence the person (agency) who controls the resource?

◆ How can your client(s) be involved in the process of securing this resource?

◆ Can/should this resource be adapted for statewide use? How would you accomplish this?

◆ Are policy changes needed? How will you advocate to get these changes made?

Successful Community Resource Development Ideas

The following strategies were generated by real-life care managers and highlight the opportunities that they have used to build on the economic assets that were already in place. The generated ideas reclaim the often-hidden treasures of a community that can be used to leverage additional community-based long-term care services.

Community Councils

Professionals in the community can join together to become part of a long-term care service committee that addresses the needs of local older adults and people with disabilities. These committees or councils can include

Health care professionals (hospital/home health)
Church/religious representatives
Area Agency on Aging care managers
Nursing facility personnel
Senior center personnel
Other clients

Senior Centers/Nutrition Sites

Resources connected with senior centers that have been developed include the following:

Meetings with interested older people to open senior centers in several communities (this includes drawing up bylaws and articles of incorporation)
Working with ministerial alliances to use volunteers for meal delivery and drivers for clients' transportation needs
Using senior centers as sites for informational programming about health and safety issues
Cooperative programming between senior centers and health departments for blood pressure checks, eye exams, and so forth

Respite Care

Volunteer training for those providing respite care in cooperation with Retired Senior Volunteer Program (RSVP)
Recruitment programs for volunteers
Project Being There—this project offers:
•Surveys of caregiver needs for congregations and businesses
•Training materials on caregiving and supportive services
•Seminars to increase clients' and families' understanding of aging issues
•Assistance in establishing a caregivers' network in a congregation or business

continued

Housing

Increased vouchers for HUD Section 8 Housing Rental Assistance Program

Community surveys of housing options for older adults

Letters of support to prospective builders from community leaders

Environmental modification grants to help make minor adjustments in older adults' homes to make them safer

Homesharing—a matched arrangement between a householder and a homeseeker to the advantage of each

Homemaker Services

Development of a homemaker program using existing nursing facility staff

Working with private homemaker services to provide discounts for low-income people

Medical Equipment

Compiled a list of agencies that loan medical equipment. List included names of contacts, telephone numbers, addresses for equipment pickup, and days available for equipment drop-off. This list will be used to develop a central location for medical equipment in a community.

Volunteer Groups

Groceries for homebound elders (donated by local grocery stores)

Handyperson services, with high school industrial education teacher as coordinator

Telephone reassurance services for homebound and lonely older people, with volunteer coordinator

Development of peer counseling

Volunteers to do paperwork for Medicaid applications and tax assistance

Operation Senior Safety—Working with volunteers from police and fire departments to provide free home safety inspections, with supplies donated from local hardware store

Transportation

Volunteers to drive older adults from their rural homes to medical appointments

Using churches to provide volunteers for a transportation club pilot project

Intergenerational Services

College workdays—helps students learn about cooperation and the rewards of volunteerism, helps older people get chores done

Youth program to involve high-school youth in providing services for older adults in their communities (e.g., homemaker services, transportation, visiting, lawn care, errands); includes extensive training and evaluation

Phone Pals—older people checking on latchkey children after school

Reverse LatchKey—children calling at-risk older people to check on their welfare

Friend-to-Friend tutoring programs connects older people with middle school–age children

References

Cox, E.O., & Parsons, R.J. (1994). *Empowerment-oriented social work practice with the elderly.* Pacific Grove: Brooks/Cole Publishing.

DeJong, P., & Miller, S.D. (1995). How to interview for client strengths. *Social Work, 40*(6), 721–864.

Epstein, L. (1988). *Helping people—The task-centered approach.* Columbus, OH: Merrill Publishing.

Fast, B., & Chapin, R. (1996). The strengths model in long term care: Linking cost containment and consumer empowerment. *Journal of Case Management, 5*(2), 51–57.

Fast, B. & Chapin, R. (1997). The strengths model with older adults: Critical practice components. In D. Saleebey (Ed.), *The strengths perspective in social work practice* (2nd ed., pp. 115–131). White Plains, NY: Longman.

Kisthardt, W.E. (1992). A strengths model of case management: The principles and functions of a helping partnership with persons with persistent mental illness. In D. Saleebey (Ed.), *The strengths perspective in social work practice* (2nd ed., pp. 59–83). White Plains, NY: Longman.

Kisthardt, W., & Rapp, C. (1992). Bridging the gap between principles and practice: Implementing a strengths perspective in case management. In S.M. Rose (Ed.), *Case management and social work practice* (pp. 112–125). Reading, MA: Addison-Wesley.

Kisthardt, W., Gowdy, E., & Rapp, C. (1992). Factors related to successful goal attainment in case management. *Journal of Case Management, 1*(4), 117.

Kivnick, H.Q. (1993, Winter/Spring). Everyday mental health: A guide to assessing life strengths. *Generations,* 13–20.

Lowry, L. (1991). *Social work with the aging.* Prospect Heights, IL: Waveland Press.

Maluccio, A. (1981). *Promoting competence in clients.* London: The Free Press.

Motenko, A.K., & Greenberg, S. (1995). Reframing dependence in old age: A position transition for families. *Social Work, 40,* 382–389.

Ory, M., Abeles, R., & Lipman, P. (1991). *Aging, health and behavior.* Newbury Park, CA: Sage Publishing.

Perkins, K. & Tice, C. (1995). A strengths perspective in practice: Older people and mental health challenges. *Journal of Gerontological Social Work, 23*(3/4), 83–98.

Poertner, J., & Ronnau, J. (1990). A strengths approach to children with emotional disabilities. In D. Saleebey (Ed.), *The strengths perspective in social work practice* (2nd ed., pp. 111–121). White Plains, NY: Longman.

Pray, J. (1992). Maximizing the patient's uniqueness and strengths: A challenge for home health care. *Social Work in Health Care, 17*(3), 71–73.

Rapp, C.A. (1998). *The strengths model: Case management with people suffering from severe and persistent mental illness.* New York: Oxford University Press.

Rapp, C., & Chamberlain, R. (1985). Case management services to the chronically mentally ill. *Social Work, 30*(5), 417–422.

Rapp, C., & Wintersteen, R. (1989). The strengths model of case management: Results from twelve demonstrations. *Psychosocial Rehabilitation Journal, 13*(1), 23–32.

Rapp, R.C., Siegal, H.A., Fisher, J.H., & Wagner, J.H. (1992). A strengths-based model of case management/advocacy: Adapting a mental health model to practice work with persons who have substance abuse problems. In R. Ashery (Ed.), *Progress and issues in case management* (Research Monograph no. 127, pp. 79–91). Rockville, MD: National Institute on Drug Abuse.

Rappaport, J.O. (1990). Research methods and the empowerment social agenda. In P. Tolan, C. Keys, F. Chertak, & J. Leonard (Eds.), *Researching community psychology issues: Theory and methods.* Washington, DC: American Psychological Association.

Rathbone-McCuan, E. (1992). Aged adult protective services clients: People of unrecognized potential. In D. Saleebey (Ed.), *The strengths perspective in social work practice* (pp. 98–110). New York: Longman.

Rodin, J., & Langer, E. (1980). Aging labels: The decline of control and the fall of self-esteem. *Journal of Social Issues, 36*(2), 12–29.

Saleebey, D. (1992). Introduction: Power in the people. In D. Saleebey (Ed.), *The strengths perspective in social work practice* (pp. 3–17). New York: Longman.

Smith, V., & Eggleston, R. (1989, Summer). Long-term care: The medical model versus the social model. *Public Welfare,* 27–29.

Sullivan, W. (1989). Community support programs in rural areas: Developing programs without walls. *Human Services in the Rural Environment, 12*(4), 19–23.

Sullivan, W. (1992). Reconsidering the environment as a helping resource. In D. Saleebey (Ed.), *The strengths perspective in social work practice* (pp. 148–157). New York: Longman.

Sullivan, W.P., & Fisher, B.J. (1994). Intervening for success: Strengths-based case management and successful aging. *Journal of Gerontological Social Work, 22*(1/2), 61–74.

Tice, C., & Perkins, K. (1996). *Mental health issues and aging: Building on the strengths of older persons.* Pacific Grove, CA: Brooks/Cole.

Weick, A. (1984). The concept of responsibility in a health model of social work. *Social Work in Health Care, 10*(2), 13–25.

Weick, A., Rapp, C., Sullivan, W.P., & Kisthardt, W. (1989). A strengths perspective for social work practice. *Social Work, 34*(4), 350–354.

Supplemental Reading

Chapin, R., Rachlin, R., Wilkinson, D., Levy, M., & Lindbloom, R. (1998). Going home. Community re-entry of light care nursing facility residents age 65 and over. *Journal of Health Care Finance, 25*(2).

Chapin, R. (1995). Social policy development: The strengths perspective. *Social Work, 40* (4).

Fast, B., & Chapin, R. (1997). The strengths model with older adults: Critical practice components. In D. Saleebey (Ed.), *The strengths perspective in social work practice* (2nd ed.). White Plains, NY: Longman.

Fast, B., & Chapin, R. (1996). The strengths model in long term care: Linking cost containment and consumer empowerment. *Journal of Case Management, 5*(2), 51–57.

Rapp, C.A. (1998). *The strengths model: Case management with people suffering from severe and persistent mental illness.* New York: Oxford University Press.